THE TREASURES OF GOD

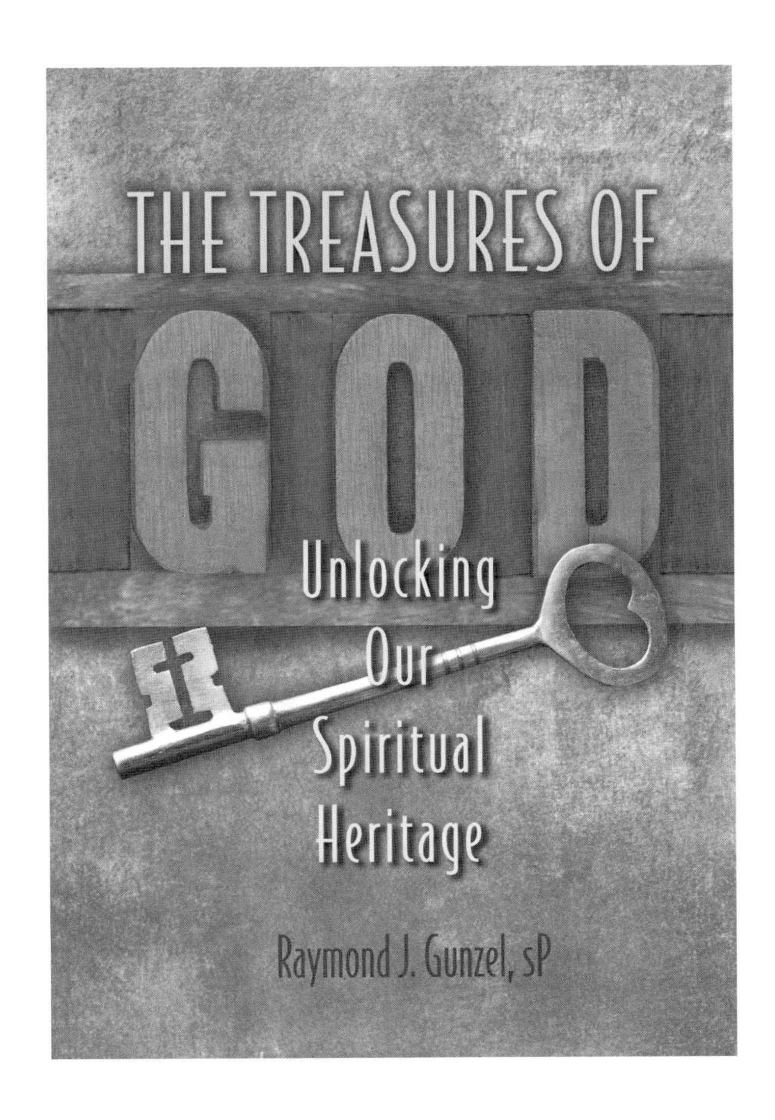

ave maria press Notre Dame, Indiana

Scripture taken from the *Holy Bible, New International Version*®. *NIV*®. Copyright © 1973, 1978, 1984 by International Bible Society. Used by permission of Zondervan Bible Publishing House. All rights reserved.

© 2002 by Ave Maria Press, Inc.

All rights reserved. No part of this book may be used or reproduced in any manner whatsoever, except in the case of reprints in the context of reviews, without written permission from Ave Maria Press, Inc., P.O. Box 428, Notre Dame, IN 46556.

www.avemariapress.com

International Standard Book Number: 0-87793-964-0

Cover and text design by Kathy Robinson Coleman

Printed and bound in the United States of America.

Library of Congress Cataloging-in-Publication Data

Gunzel, Raymond J.

The treasures of God : unlocking our spiritual heritage/Raymond J. Gunzel.

p. cm.

ISBN 0-87793-964-0 (pbk.)

1. Spiritual life--Catholic Church. 2. Prayer. I. Title.

BX2350.3 .G86 2002

248.3--dc21

2001008128

CIP

Contents

Foreword

"Prayer is the opening of the mind and heart to God." Thus the Baltimore Catechism introduced the faithful to a conscious intimate relationship with God; a relationship that few fully realized. Few understood the incredible depths of the mystery of their relationship with God contained in these few simple words. Opening, or lifting, our mind and heart to God speaks of a process of standing, waiting, expecting. It implies a notion of being in the presence of a mystery that transcends the horizons of our everyday consciousness. It is the action of faith that moves beyond words and formulas to a readiness to be filled, taken into a relationship that would transform us and alter our experience of life. As we pray, so we live. If the actions, words, and rituals we use in prayer lead to an opening of the heart and mind to God, all our actions, thoughts, and relationships become an expression of this relationship.

Couched in this definition is a formula for union with God enjoyed by the mystics of all traditions throughout the ages. In this formula we discover the seed-bed of our ancient and venerable tradition of Christian contemplative prayer. It follows that this formula places us in a relationship with the countless men and women of all traditions who have sought union with God in whatever way they understood that term.

It is not an exaggeration to say that this formula defines all prayer as contemplative, mystical openness to union with the divine. Contemplative prayer is here understood to be that simple resting in the experience of God's immediate presence deep within our soul.

Silently, without words, desire, or thought we stop all activity to simply savor God's presence awakened by the words of our prayer or the actions of our ritual. Our Judeo-Christian understanding of God coming from sacred scripture as well as the experience of the faith community through the ages is that God created us for a personal relationship in order that we might receive and become bearers of divine love and wisdom. To open to the full meaning of this definition of prayer is to allow ourselves to be drawn into the mystery of divine love nested within our deep inner self. It is to be drawn into the mystery of the forgotten truth of our human nature, to have been created out of the earth and breathed into life by the breath of the divinity (Gn 2:7). This is an experience that is available to all without exception. No one can teach us how to pray, we do not have to learn how to pray. Rather we have to learn how to release ourselves from our inhibition, our fears, our need to control, to do it right, and allow our hearts to escape into their longed-for union with the divine Abba.

I do not lay claim to any ability to teach anyone to pray. That is not my intention in writing this brief book on prayer. And lest anyone believe that this is a book on how to pray, let me disabuse them of that notion at the beginning. The basic premise of this book is that the human person is created as a praying being. Prayer is "hard-wired" into our being and our heart innately drives us to seek union with God, the ground of our being. Thus, in our union with God we find the truth of our personal existence.

We do not have to learn how to pray, rather we have to set ourselves about the task of discarding the inhibitions and deceptions that we have gathered along the way as we forged a personality created in the image and likeness of our culture, our family, our social environment, possibly even our religious heritage. Yes, even religion can be co-opted into the service of maintaining our cultural value system. We need to reclaim our immediate and personal relationship with a God who wants to draw us into divine union, a union that cleanses and heals. What I would like to accomplish in this book is to encourage readers to trust the innate goodness and holiness of their human nature in a way that allows the prayer of their heart to come forth and express itself in a natural and simple way. Readers are asked to get in touch with the various ways in which their hearts are urging them to connect with the truth of their personhood, to trust their intuitive leaning toward God.

For most of our lifetime, many of us considered prayer to be a dutiful recitation of pre-set formulas offered to a God who took note of the faithful fulfillment of our religious obligation—or noted the lack of such fulfillment. For many, the life of prayer and devotions was grounded in a subtle fear of offending a judgmental God who was all too ready to punish those who did not "get it right." God was similar to a beloved but feared old grandfather whose role in our lives was to see to it that we behaved and kept the rules. We did not expect, much less did we desire, an experience of loving immediacy to God. This was left to those living in the cloister, far removed from the distractions of daily life in the world. For the rest of us, God was best kept at a safe distance.

Nor did we believe that prayer was a necessary component of a healthy and well balanced emotional, social, and psychological life. We did not believe—perhaps we did not want to believe—that true prayer is a passage into a bold and mature engagement with the mysteries and conundrums of life. For the most part prayer was our connection to God who lived beyond time and space, a duty to prepare for our ultimate life with God in the hereafter delivered from the burdens and cares of this life. Our task on the way was to get things ordered so that we could escape the feared wrath and ultimate disapproval of this grandfather in the sky. We were content to fulfill our duties faithfully, endure our struggles stoically, and await our reward in the next life, hoping that when the time came we would pass muster. We understood this life to be a radical separation from God and a preparation for full union with God that could only be fully enjoyed in the next life.

For many others prayer opened up a space wherein we could momentarily escape the burdens and trials of daily existence and perhaps capture a glimpse of the peace of a cosmic Santa Claus who indulged, in fact encouraged, our perpetual infancy. God was at best a dysfunctional parent who ruled either by fear and intimidation or by whimsical and self-serving indulgence. This dysfunctional God is in fact a creature of our own making, the God of our impoverished and truncated imagination. We enjoyed a relationship with a safe God who might have punished for petty infractions or rewarded our childish offerings, but who never challenged us beyond the safe and cozy boundaries of our carefully crafted zone of security and personal comfort. Ours was a God who was content with our idle and sometimes bored Sunday pittance.

Contrast this God of our own image and likeness to the God of Moses, Abraham and Sarah, the God of the prophets and the God of Jesus Christ and his immediate disciples. This is the God who penetrated and disrupted the lives of saints and prophets down through the ages to our own time. This is the God who called Martin Luther King to put his life on the line for a more just society for all, the God who enticed Dorothy Day to a life spent in the service of the poor, the God who took Mahatma Gandhi from the possibility of a comfortable life as a barrister to one of unending suffering and ultimate martyrdom for the poor and oppressed of his nation. The God we know from our tradition is a God who enters into our lives and stretches us beyond all known or imagined horizons of our imagination to become prophets, mystics and yes, martyrs, in bringing about the Kingdom of God on earth right here and now in our time and place, within the confines of our family, friends, and coworkers. The God of our tradition is not one who encourages us to abandon the world, forget the struggles of our brothers and sisters toward justice, and to ignore the steadily increasing plight of creation. Rather our God is a God of creation and history who has called us to care for one another and creation, to spend our lives building a world of justice and peace for creatures. Many have turned religion and its beliefs and practices into an enterprise of narcissistic self-absorption, constantly seeking consolation and comfort, but with little awareness or concern for the fundamental and core gospel value of selfless service. In contrast to much that passes for therapy today, the gospel holds up self-forgetfulness and service as a remedy for much of what ails us.

And all this begins when we open our hearts and minds to God in our humble prayer. In our eagerness to know a god of consolation and comfort, we lost sight of the fact that God must first disrupt and dismantle in order to reveal the peace and joy of the divine presence, to transform us into sacraments of peace, justice, compassion, and reconciliation.

It has remained beyond the hope of most of us to live a life of contemplative union with God, a union that permeated, purified, and transformed our perceptions, elevated our thoughts, and sanctified our relationships here and now. Few of us realized that through this unifying action our joys and sorrows were to be made one, actually, with the sacrifice of Jesus, one with the paschal mystery and therefore one with the joys and sufferings of our human family. Through our prayers, solitary as well as communal, we participate in the redemption and transformation of our world. Prayer was certainly not seen as a process of discovering our innate holiness, the sacred and god-like qualities buried deep within our heart center, much less did we see it as a path to discover our lost and abandoned heroism.

We can understand then why easy, superficial prayer might be the preference of many; prayer, true prayer, according to our definition, is a fearsome enterprise. It opens us to embrace the responsibility of becoming fully individuated and responsible adults. Mature adults accept responsibility for their relationship with God; they are ready to engage in a mature and adult relationship with a God who created us to fully participate in the creation and redemption of the world. But like any relationship, our relationship with God requires change, moving out of secure places in order to discover the wider horizons and greater depths of our human potential.

In the years since Vatican Council II there has been a steadily increasing interest in the contemplative traditions of the non-Christian East. This has not been seen by most as a negation of Christianity since many—perhaps most—Christians who have explored the prayer forms of these traditions have remained for the most part actively engaged in their Christian tradition. It is significant that many of the teachers from the East testify that a significant number of those coming to Eastern meditation practice seem to be Roman Catholics and Jews. There is also a significant representation of Episcopalians and Lutherans with a smattering of representatives from other Protestant sects.

I believe there is a reason for the significant numbers of Roman Catholics, Episcopalians, and Lutherans among the seekers going to the East to discover methods and disciplines of contemplation. Because these Christian traditions have maintained their essential liturgical and sacramental character, there is by necessity an element of mystery hidden within the sacramental images and symbolic actions of these traditions. These traditions have by the very fact of the liturgical and sacramental character the implication of something more, something beneath the actions of the liturgy, something hidden that cannot be comprehended by the rational mind or by the force of the human will. There is a call to penetrate the mystery being conveyed by means other than one's normal state of consciousness, beyond the capacity of our mind and will. The liturgy, the images, the rituals of the church convey and transmit a meaning and a mystery that one must open oneself to on a level deeper than the rational mind. The message of Christ is a message conveyed to the heart, and only the heart can hear the true meaning of the words and actions of Jesus Christ made present in our lives through sacrament and liturgy. Only the heart can reveal the true and deeper meaning of Christ to our mind and bring about transformed actions and relationships.

Christianity is a contemplative and mystical religion aimed at bringing about the transformation of the human heart, the clearing and purification of our mind in order that we might see, hear, and act with the mind and heart of Christ. This contemplative and mystical aspect of our tradition is couched within the rituals, symbols, and images of the liturgy and sacraments. Christianity is not a religion of doing as much as it is a religion of being and becoming a new creation in Christ. Our effective doing in the world can only emerge from a renewed consciousness cleansed from the toxic influences of an unenlightened culture. When these essentially contemplative, mystical faith traditions lose their connection to the life-giving core and settle for an emphasis on mind and will, the true meaning behind the rituals is lost and they become empty gestures. When the inner meaning of rituals, images, and sacraments is lost and rational thought and willful action are substituted for contemplative knowing, the heart is tantalized without being truly nourished.

The result is that many begin to wander in search of food that challenges and sticks to the ribs. Others wonder why their heart remains so untouched by their religious belief and practice. As I observed before and will continue to say, Christianity is essentially a revelation that speaks to the heart. Contemplation is the passageway that leads to the heart and soul of our revelation, the very heart of God. A renewed consciousness is the fruit of entering into the heart of God through Christ, a mystical openness to perceive the mystery of God continually self-giving through creation and the life of each human person.

Over the past several centuries the Western world has become increasingly fascinated and enamored by the power of the mind and will. This is not a bad thing, nor are the mind and will to be denigrated or despised in the search for the deeper meaning of the Christian mystery. However, the mind and will alone are not capable of comprehending the full depth and breadth of the mystery of Christ. There are also intuition and affect. When we speak of divine revelation being addressed to the heart center, we mean that divine revelation addresses itself to the entire person, mind, will, intuition, and affect, even to having a substantial effect on our body. We have to allow the Word to pass through the mind and penetrate to the deep of our interior life, the center where our life and the life of the divine merge and become one, where the division between time and eternity, matter and spirit dissolve. This is the place where our inner hunger and longings originate. It is the only place where they can be satisfied.

This is the place where the mystics discovered themselves to be one with God and one with creation and the entire human family; where they passed beyond the veils of one-dimensional perceptions into the awakened state in which they realized that all was ultimately one with the divine. In a variety of ways they attempted to help us understand that their experience was available for all. For Catholics and other liturgical and sacramental traditions, it is our sacraments, our rituals, and our images that are intended to lead us to this clarification of mind and heart, this openness that enables us to enter into the mystery. In this mystery we become one with the mind and heart of Christ and live in union with the Creator of all and find our oneness with all other people and creation as well. When we allow our prayer disciplines and rituals to draw us into the heart center, prayer restores us to a wholeness that unites mind, heart, soul, and spirit with body. This is the true fruit of prayer. When our hearts are opened in expectant listening, our rituals, formulas and words awaken the eternal prayer embedded there. When on the other hand, our prayer formulas and rituals remain on the external level, a mere exercise of mind and will, our inner life of the spirit languishes, the prayer sleeping within our heart center remains unheeded.

This contemplative, mystical core has been kept alive and available in our monastic traditions. However, generally speaking—and this is true to some extent even of the monastic experience up until recent years—the Western Christian church has paid only lip service to our contemplative or mystical tradition. We have substituted theories of spirituality for the experience of personal, deep spirituality. Western Christianity has been largely a church of "doing" religion, without sufficient encouragement being given to penetrate beneath the surface of the practice to the wellsprings of the contemplative and mystical tradition.

The following pages are admittedly a modest and incomplete attempt to explain some of the basic principles and practices that nourish our growth into a contemplative—that is, fully awake—life of prayer and active life in the world. For this reason I have included a very brief, but adequate, reading list at the end of the book. This list will provide the reader with sufficient material to gain a fairly comprehensive knowledge of various methods of contemplative prayer. There is no substitute for personal practice, however. The point is to begin a faithful daily practice to allow one's inner life to open. Over time prayer grows in us and develops a life of its own, leading us to deeper wisdom and self-knowledge. We begin to experience God as a vital presence in our everyday lives and actions.

It is my hope that the reader may be further motivated to take seriously the heart's natural longing for a deeper intimacy with the Divine, and for a more meaningful and creative engagement in the tasks of daily life in the world. Indeed a natural desire for deeper prayer, a more immediate experience of God is not something to be brushed aside and dismissed as a whimsical fantasy, but rather should be recognized, acknowledged, and nurtured. It is a desire authored by God and kept alive by the Holy Spirit. We ignore these inner promptings to our peril.

Once we respond to this natural inclination for a deeper interior life, sacred scripture comes alive in a surprisingly new way. We discover that the Hebrew scriptures and the life of Christ call us to a transformation of consciousness and a renewal of attitudes and behaviors that can only come from a heart that is opened and liberated to free its prayer and to perceive reality in an entirely new way.

I attempt to present contemplative prayer and mindful living in a way that is a challenge requiring a commitment and a willingness to let go of many conventional attitudes about the Christian life, our life of prayer and worship. But with the challenges, it is accessible to anyone motivated by a strong conviction that there is more to religion and faith than the mere repetition of rituals and adherence to codes of belief.

I have made an effort to avoid the false promise of shallow consolation and painless bliss. In fact I have made a conscious effort to make the reader aware of the serious challenges involved in the contemplative path. However, I hope I have made it equally clear that our common call to follow Christ is nothing less than a call to radical inner transformation that is the fruit of contemplative prayer.

Contemplative prayer and conscious living put us on a path that leads to truth and liberation from the delusions of a one-dimensional world and a one-dimensional and hollow religiosity; self-serving and ultimately self-defeating. To get beneath this level opens us to the trials of purification and a liberation from deeply imbedded delusions and false assumptions which we might have come to accept as normal.

God is truth. Jesus Christ is the definitive revelation of the inner mystery of God. Jesus is also, by that very fact, the definitive revelation of our own inner, core truth. We are, after all, each uniquely created to reveal God's divine image in our life. To truly know Jesus is to know who we truly are, what we are called to be, and how we are called to act. To accept the call to follow Jesus is to embark on a path that will lead us into the lost, hidden truth of our own true selves.

Jesus ultimately leads us to the truth and freedom of the resurrection, but that way leads through the darkness of not knowing and the purification of all that is not true and holy in our lives. For those who have labored to believe that the darkness of our one-dimensional world is, instead, light and truth and that the foolishness of conventional understanding is wisdom, the process of awakening to truth, seeing the light for the first time, can be painful and disorienting. I remember with a bone-chilling shudder the moment I awakened to the soul shaking awareness that I was not, after all these years and effort, the person I had believed myself to be; I was not the person I had so fondly wished others to believe I was. As I felt the very bottom fall from beneath me I wondered who I was. Was there really anything left? If I was not this carefully crafted person, this meticulously constructed persona who conscientiously embodied all the virtues that our society and church so cherished, who was I? In a fog of bewilderment bordering on despair, I fumbled my way to the scriptures and turned the pages seeking some light. Like a blast of lightning in the midst of a black night, Psalm 139 found its way into the depths of my heart.

> For you created my inmost being; you knit me together in my mother's womb.
>
> I praise you because I am fearfully and wonderfully made; your works are wonderful, I know that full well.
>
> My frame was not hidden from you when I was made in the secret place. When I was woven together in the depths of the earth, your eyes saw my unformed body.
>
> All the days ordained for me were written in your book before one of them came to be (vv. 13-16).

This passage opened my heart and not only the prayer of the psalmist poured into my being, but also the heartfelt prayer of every searching, longing human being who ever cried out for meaning and understanding. Past, present, and future called out at once. I experienced then the unshakable conviction that every prayer that has ever been uttered, every prayer that will ever be uttered, no matter how beautiful or how humble and trite, is embedded within my heart and every heart, awaiting its birth into song, dance, praise, and contrition. Each time I pray, each time I celebrate the eucharist, I open my heart not only to God, but I also open my heart to the unheard, unspoken prayer of every human heart. I do not go to God alone, but in a procession of countless human souls looking for God, even when they don't know or acknowledge what they are looking for. In my prayer, their prayer finds expression; in their darkness, their suffering, in their sinfulness, my prayer finds its ground.

In my prayer there is carried the prayer of every human person. The lost, unrecognized, distorted, and anguished prayer of the abandoned is in my heart. The prayer of the most abject sinner or the most exalted saint awaits its word, its formula, and its heartfelt expression through my utterance. As my prayer opens my heart, readying it to be joined with the Spirit and carried to the heart of Jesus Christ, so too is the prayer of every creature on earth, perhaps most especially the unheard and anguished prayer of the prostitute, the outcast, and the death row inmate. If my prayer can carry their cry to God, their lived reality remains the ground that keeps me connected to the reality of our commonly shared human condition. When sacred scripture, the liturgy, and the sacraments open my heart to release the prayer within, then the prayer of all creation—especially the prayer of the most abandoned—finds its way into the heart of God.

As we persevere over time, we come to realize that living our lives anchored in the Divine Word brings us closer to our true identity in Jesus Christ who lives through his Spirit and joins us to one another. Living in Jesus Christ through his Spirit, we come to know ourselves for the first time. We come to know and understand that we are not alone, we are not separate from one another, but joined in a profound and radically true and substantial way to one another and to all creation in the one life of God in Christ.

This effort is aimed primarily at that large body of Christians who are devoted to their church and its beliefs and practices, but who perhaps remain unaware of the enormous depth of mystery lying just beneath the surface. However, even though I speak of traditions and practices that are common to Roman Catholics, I do not intend to exclude members of other traditions.

The Catholic church has been the custodian of such practices as the rosary, stations of the cross, the Jesus prayer, and countless other forms of prayer that have become identified with being "Roman." The truth is, however, that these practices convey through time and across cultures universal truths that speak to the heart of every human person, that open the way to a deep and personal union with God. The church does not own them, it holds them out for anyone who is seriously looking for a way into the heart of God. Therefore, I hope and pray that many within other faith traditions might be encouraged to come and see for themselves how our ancient shared faith draws us together in our common hunger for union with the divine. Just as many of us have wandered and grazed in other fields, so now I hope and pray that many Christians will come to taste and see what has been waiting for them right in their own back yard.

Throughout this book I will insist that all our beliefs and devotional practices are aimed at leading each person to a personal and immediate encounter with God through Jesus Christ. In that union we know what it means to be a person created in the image and likeness of God. Most fundamentally, we know specifically what it means to be the person we are, born in this time, with this name, as a husband or wife, mother or father, friend, lover in a specific time and place with a particular set of circumstances. The very ground of our being is the divine image in which we are created. This is the source of our insatiable hunger and thirst. This hunger and thirst, however, is vulnerable to easy seduction by the gods of our consumer society that glorifies greed and easy gratification, even, I might add, in things religious.

The first five chapters of the book deal with more general principles of our contemplative tradition. I hope to lay the foundations upon which we can then move to more specific considerations of a contemplative prayer practice. I attempt to demonstrate that all life—and every experience of life—is a means of encountering the divine. The more specific practices are the means by which we sensitize our heart to the abiding presence of God in every nook and cranny of our daily life.

The Word of God is the keystone of the spiritual life of the Christian. Therefore I suggest that the ancient tradition of *lectio divina,* understood as a prayerful reading of sacred scripture, is the foundation of our prayer life. *Lectio* allows the soul to open itself to be penetrated, enlightened and healed by God's eternal Word. It is the Word that must become our guide through the struggles and seductive temptations of this life. The sections on the Jesus Prayer, Centering Prayer, the Rosary, and the Stations of the Cross attempt to show how these traditional devotions are alternative and easily accessible ways to open ourselves to God's Word. I hope to show that these common devotions are nothing if not gateways to deep contemplative prayer and mystical union with the divine right here and now. These practices and devotions transcend denominational and creedal boundaries and are ways into the very heart of the Christ event, being in fact "catholic" in the truest sense of that word.

Following this, readers are invited to reflect on a contemplative approach to the eucharist—the very centerpiece of our faith and the primary source of our spiritual nourishment. The eucharist brings together in one sacramental form the entire mystery of the divine Word in our life.

Finally I encourage readers to think seriously about the place of sacred time in their lives; time that is dedicated to the soul's nourishment. I encourage activities that take them away from the normal routine of the workaday world and allow readers to explore the creative and intuitive side of their lives. Sabbath time should be a time in which life is restored and reconnected to deeper wellsprings; it is not an imperative imposed from without, but rather one that comes from within, calling us to connect with our own inner innate wisdom.

It is my hope and prayer that in this era of intense spiritual seeking, people will be made aware of the oftentimes forgotten or ignored fact that, at its best, the church is a vessel of an enormous bounty of contemplative mystical riches available for all who seek. Jesus' call to each of us is to follow him on a path that leads from spiritual and psychological captivity to ultimate freedom in God. The freedom and union with God can be ours, here, now, in the midst of our daily lives and human relationships. In Christ, we can become living sacraments of healing and redemption for our time, even as we continue to struggle in our own experience of sinfulness and human frailty.

The effort of this introduction to contemplative prayer and mysticism is driven by both sadness and hope. First, sadness at the sight of so many Christians who seek true prayer and union with God outside our faith tradition and practice. Many, including myself, have been greatly enriched and spiritually nourished by such exploration, and have come full circle back to our roots with a deeper appreciation of our own contemplative and mystical tradition. Many others, however, remain unaware of the deep spiritual treasures they have left behind. Tragically, many pastors and teachers themselves remain on the surface of the devotional practice of the church and are therefore unable to lead others to where they themselves have not been.

In the end, however, it is hope that motivates the effort; hope and confidence lead me to believe that the time has now come when large numbers of Christians of all traditions—laity, clergy, and religious—are going to look deeper into their everyday religious practices and beliefs. Looking deeper, they will recognize and respond to their inner call to find their personal and unique place at the banquet table.

When we return to our contemplative and mystical depths, a new fire will be released upon the earth. Our Christian faith will catch fire in the everyday lives of engaged contemplatives and mystics. Through their lives the church will be the agent of transformation in and through Christ living and acting in and through the actions of the praying faithful.

I remind the reader that, after all, this book is merely a prod, an invitation to live life more deeply. In the end the reader will have to decide whether or not to lay aside all doubts and hesitations and take the first step into a daily encounter with the living God. It is only in the doing that one will realize that God is waiting to meet us in our effort and, through the Spirit living within us, lead us to where we could never imagine we could go, to do that which we never believed possible, to experience what we had thought reserved to others.

It is my prayer and hope that this book will provide a tantalizing taste that will entice one to further explorations into our deep and ancient heritage of contemplative prayer and mystical awareness of the living God accompanying us on our journey through life.

Finally I believe that as Christians discover their call to be truly transformed in Christ, to become a new creation, God's mighty presence in history will again break through into our lives and into the world. We will again be a redeeming force leading humanity and creation to its appointed end.

one

God's Word Is Alive

In the Christian tradition contemplative prayer is the normal fruit of the regular practice of reflecting on the Word of God. Most commonly the Word is encountered in a prayerful reading of sacred scripture traditionally referred to as *lectio divina*. The practice of *lectio* originated in the ancient monasteries where the monks sought, by continual repetition, to become so one with the Word that it became a habitual presence in their consciousness. This presence was an active and dynamic one that had a specific effect on their lives and the way they understood themselves as persons. The expected result was that their consciousness became completely suffused with an awareness of God's living Word present in them. The praying of the Word continued to resonate in their consciousness even as they went about their daily labors and sometimes even continued in their sleep. This was accomplished not only by the singing of the psalms and readings of the Office several times a day, but by personal reading and study. As the results of this practice were observed over many generations it was discovered that there was a process by which each monk, with diligent and patient perseverance, was led to a contemplative resting with the Word in the heart beyond thought or images. The Word became an abiding and habitual presence with the result that their lives and relationships were transformed; they became the Word they prayed. They divided this process into four different stages leading from the beginning, *lectio* through *meditatio*, *oratio*, and finally *contemplatio*, resting with the Word in the heart. Thus *contemplatio*, contemplation, was understood as being the expected fruit of diligent and regular prayerful reading of sacred scripture. It was an experience open to anyone who prayerfully approached the Word with trust and perseverance. It was not an uncommon experience for a monk to be in a habitual state of contemplation.

Today we understand *lectio divina* to be the formal and ritualized reading of a passage, preferably short, from sacred scripture. A regular and disciplined daily reading of sacred scripture sensitizes us to the wisdom and relevancy of God's Word in our daily life. As time goes on and a person becomes more spiritually sensitive to the presence of God in everyday life and creation, deep contemplative moments may arise out of any event or circumstance. The fruit of a regular discipline of contemplative prayer is a mind and heart opened to perceive and honor the presence of God in every aspect of daily life. We live and act in a conscious awareness of the sacred quality of even the least of our daily actions. So even today the grace of contemplative union with God's living Word is available to anyone who finds the motivation to engage this ancient spiritual discipline with trust and perseverance. Throughout the course of this book I hope to show how all our religious practices ultimately lead us to a relationship with God's living Word. Later we will treat the practice of *lectio* in more detail and then attempt to show how other common practices are simply alternative ways to encountering the Word. Before we attempt this, however, it will be helpful to take the time to consider more general principles relating to our practice of prayer. This will help us understand that ultimately all our actions that come under the rubric of prayer have as their ultimate goal contemplative union with the divine. And it needs to be said that this union brings about a transformation of consciousness which gives us a new way of understanding what it means to be a human being, a person within a constellation of relationships.

In childhood, when we first began to recite the words of the Our Father, the Hail Mary, and other formal prayers and public liturgical celebrations, we were setting off on a spiritual journey that was intended to form our consciousness and create a unique Christian identity, to live in Christ. We were established in a relationship with God and the saints as well as the universal faith community, past, present and future. The words, images, celebrations, and symbols of our religious practice provided us with a story and tradition that placed us in a community that extended through history and across geographical, cultural, and national boundaries. All the images, rituals, celebrations, and stories provided us with a way of connecting ourselves to an extended religious family with common beliefs, a shared way of understanding the world and our place within it. We were given a purpose and destiny that revealed within us a sense of being in relationship with a wisdom and a nurturing presence that guided us and protected us, that gave us a purpose and a reason for being.

The religious beliefs and practices learned from our earliest childhood place us within a network of relationships that stretch back through history to the dawn of religious awakening. Our religious consciousness and strivings place our hearts within the universal human experience of restlessly searching for meaning and purpose. This is a characteristic that is shared by all men and women of every age and place. This restless search, this longing, is the seed bed of spirituality. When this longing awakens within us we have joined the great company of men and women down through the centuries—shamans and medicine people, seers and oracles, prophets and mystics, and the faithful of our own day—who have recognized and acknowledged the call to seek something larger and more lasting than the fleeting satisfactions of the material world alone.

The great religious traditions have been formed by the many great teachers who have embarked on this ageless human quest. For this reason our great religious traditions are sources of human unity, not sources of division and enmity. The Judeo-Christian tradition takes its place among the world religions as a tradition that offers the way into the full meaning of what it means to be a human person seeking ultimate unity with the divine. Our tradition is unique in that it focuses our search for truth and ultimate meaning not in the far reaches of space, but in a vital and creative engagement in the unfolding of the created universe. Our life and meaning continue from where God rested on the seventh day.

The stories of Abraham and Sarah, Moses and the chosen people of Israel connect us to the rest of humanity and our commonly shared quest for meaning. This unfolding story of God's mercy enabled our ancestors to hope in something that knit together the various strands of life into a meaningful pattern. Faith in something larger and wiser than themselves carried our ancestors through their struggles, challenges, failures, and tragedies. Faith forged their identity and gave them a purpose and destiny. The belief that God was with them in their daily lives and struggles provided an anchor from which they could hope and trust. Against the pain and trials of everyday life, they could place the promise of a Savior, a redeemer who would eventually deliver them into a promised land.

You and I today stand on the ground they cultivated. From this ground of faith, our lives touch and influence the lives of others. From this ground our lives open up and reach into the future, where our beliefs and actions will flower into something totally new and unknown, unimagined by us today. Just as we stand today and receive the wisdom gained from the struggles of past generations, so will a future generation look back on us as their matriarchs and patriarchs, their mystics, prophets, and heroes whose faith is their heritage, the source of their strength. Through our faith-filled action today we will have handed to them a body of beliefs and practices that anchor life in a reality not affected by the shifting sands of our historical passage.

Our lives are at the intersection of four great currents of spiritual energy. First, we are the products of the past, energized by the wisdom gained by the struggles, longings, and aspirations of our ancient mothers and fathers. Second, our lives are touched and influenced by the events and circumstances of our present time. Likewise, inspired by sacred scripture and the living tradition of our faith community, our lives touch and influence our own time and place as it opens into the future. Third, God, through the Holy Spirit, guides and inspires this intersection of past, present, and future. God directs that our lives reach into eternity to touch and be touched by the communion of saints. Our lives are sacramental; through them, God's transformative action is mediated to our world. Fourth, our participation in a faith community, our personal and communal prayer, and our openness to the eternal and transcendent God acting in our time and place mediate our opening to the Spirit. We attend to God's spirit speaking to us now through the signs of our time and place in history. The unfolding of divine revelation continues in the Holy Spirit as we search for meaning and understanding in our communal life. We must always remember that it is our personal relationship with God that enriches the life of the community. Our faith tradition does not lead us to a life separate from this historical moment, but rather through our relationship with the divine here and now, we become the connecting link that unites time with eternity, heaven with earth. I want to emphasize that the quality of our relationship with God determines the quality of our ability to be instruments of divine grace in our time and place.

Our relationship with God at this present time enables us to apply the wisdom of past ages in a way that nourishes and energizes our present faith community. We then become agents, sacraments of spiritual energy for our time. Because the future is built on the ground of the present, the quality of our lived faith today becomes our gift to future generations.

As we mature into adulthood with a faith nurtured by these four points of intersection with divine wisdom, we interiorize the meaning of the stories and rituals, the laws and traditions. Thus we experience the formation of a consciousness and establish a self-reference with a world-view radically different than if we hadn't been exposed to these influences. Religion is essentially a consciousness altering experience. Religion's stories, images, rituals and symbols provide us with a context within which to face the mysteries, challenges, and puzzles of life. Our personal spiritual searching, nurtured and formed by our religious story, ritual, and devotions, becomes our gift of new possibilities for our time and place. Our life lived in faith becomes the transforming spiritual energy that redirects our spiritual passage toward its proper end.

Our faith story tells us that all creation is the unfolding of divine wisdom and stands as the first and primary revelation of God's creative Word. Awe and wonder at the presence and action of God in our lives and creation are the soul's response to grace as the Word unfolds its deeper meaning, revealing the truth of God's presence in love within us as well as in creation and history.

In recent years many have understood and experienced religion and religious practices as closing off their spiritual life from the current of life around them, especially the dynamic flow of life in creation. In fact our rituals and ceremonies have their roots in the seasons and rhythms of creation and the cycles and epochs as well as the very concrete experiences of human life. The sacraments themselves have the capacity to open our eyes and hearts to the presence of God in the most basic experiences of our bodily life connected to the earth and our bodily sensations. Consequently, our life of faith is aimed at opening our awareness to the presence of the sacred in every dimension of our life on earth. This touches on a neglected, misunderstood aspect of our spirituality. Namely, Christian spirituality is sensual; it evokes feeling, a physical response to God as beauty, truth, and goodness. We are closest to God when the entire body, mind, and spirit come together in an ecstatic response to a presence that penetrates our deepest self and opens us to experience our very concrete connection to all creation. Insofar as we are alienated from our body and sense of the sacred in the dynamic beauty of creation, our contemplation remains sterile and arid and we deny ourselves the ecstatic quality of our spirituality.

Standing in contemplative silence and solitude before creation, the soul awakens to an awareness of

God's living presence within and rests in wordless silence beyond thought and imagination. The Word we have read and prayed, either in sacred scripture, creation, or in our lived experience, reveals the truth nested within the depths of our soul. We experience in our lives the mystery of the eternal Word of God, the Word that transcends history, space, and cultures, encountering its unique expression in our lives. Each of us is an utterance of the divine. The unique enfleshed existence of each human life gives a particular manifestation to the inner life of God, in whose image we are created. The Word of God in sacred scripture, nested in creation and within the folds of our inner self, reveals the pure truth of what we were created to be in the mind of God. Through contemplative prayer, our heart gradually awakens to consciously acknowledge and embrace this reality as the foundation of our identity.

> The word of God is living and active. Sharper than any double-edged sword, it penetrates even to dividing soul and spirit, joints and marrow; it judges the thoughts and attitudes of the heart. Nothing in all creation is hidden from God's sight. Everything is uncovered and laid bare before the eyes of him to whom we must give account (Heb 4:12-13).

Christian contemplative prayer is firmly anchored in a living trust and faith in God's active and living presence in sacred scripture, and in a similar fashion, in all creation. "The spirit of God was, hovering over the waters. And God said, 'let there be . . .' and there was . . ." (Cf. Gn 1:2-26). This passage from Genesis relates in a mythopoetic way how the early mystic poets understood the creative potency of God's creative power. In the Semitic understanding, the word had the power to bring into existence what it spoke. "God said, and so it was. . . ."

God's Word calls creation into being as a revelation of the inner life of God. In John's gospel we read:

> In the beginning was the Word, and the Word was with God, and the Word was God. He was with God in the beginning.
>
> Through him all things were made; without him nothing was made that has been made. In him was life, and that life was the light of men. The light shines in the darkness, but the darkness has not understood it (Jn 1:1-5).

In John's mystic, poetic way, he is telling us that within the darkness and "not-knowing" of our one-dimensional awareness, there is nested the eternal and ineradicable truth of God's inner wisdom, the truth of the "Word" that is one with the truth of God. Each of us, in fact all creation, is in our own way a word spoken, a revelation of the inner mystery of God who speaks and self-reveals through creation. Creation manifests the inner wisdom of God. Insofar as we allow the Word of sacred scripture—and all revealed truth—to penetrate and open our consciousness to the truth of God within us, we become truly human, truly the persons God created us to be. We live in light, the light that dispels the darkness. When our life and action are freed from darkness, we become manifestations of the divine.

The fruit of contemplative prayer is a soul opened and penetrated, filled with an abiding awareness of God's life and action in creation, but most particularly in the lived experience of the person. The soul sees in every being, human and non-human, a manifestation of the handiwork of God. Contemplation is the liberation of the human mind from the illusion of a static, one-dimensional material universe, to behold the presence and creative action of God, begun when God said: "Let there be . . ."

We can perhaps begin to see now that when Jesus responded to his disciples' plea to "teach us to pray," Jesus opened a process that would lead to a new consciousness. He showed them a new way of perceiving the world, themselves in the world, and themselves in relation to God and one another. To pray as Jesus taught is to begin a journey that leads us to a new way of seeing and living in the world, a way that confounds and confuses the conventional way of living in and understanding the world. We become a people who see with new eyes, hear with new ears, and understand with a renewed mind. We will explore more deeply the prayer that Jesus taught his disciples in a later chapter.

two

Compassion for All Beings

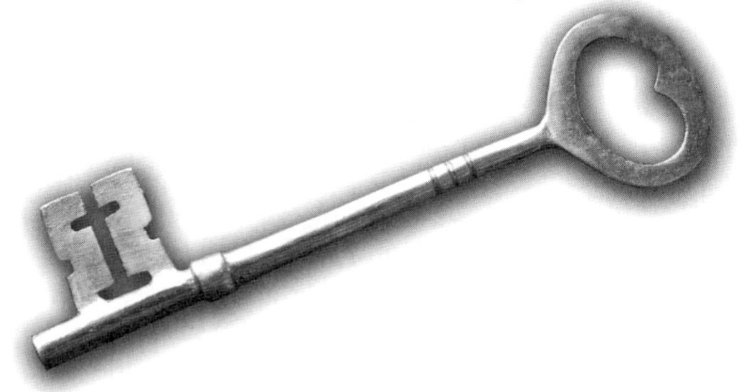

Before we talk about the specific disciplines and practices associated with contemplative prayer, we need to understand these terms within a context of spirituality that is relational. Prayer is essentially a process of expanding relationships, moving from our heart center to a relationship of love, compassion, and justice for all beings. Prayer is definitely not a unilateral, one-on-one relationship between ourselves and God. Prayer does not begin and end with the completion of words or rituals of worship. We relate to God from within the context of an entire spectrum of relationships including ourselves, our neighbor, and creation. Prayer and worship are not complete until they bear fruit in renewed and healed relationships, beginning with ourselves and extending to include all members of the human family and the world around us, including material and non-human beings.

Western Christianity has been seriously harmed by a notion that religion and spirituality are meant to disengage us from concerns about our life on earth and the well-being of the earth. Many have the mistaken notion that religion is all about the "afterlife," somewhere else at a later time. Our tradition from the very beginning is one that heavily involves us in the unfolding of creation, the sanctification of history, and the well-being of human persons. It is not an exaggeration to say that to believe that we can have a relationship with God while ignoring the condition of the earth and the well-being of other persons is seriously delusional. We don't need to look far to see the serious damage this kind of "otherworldly" religious belief and practice has brought upon our society and our world.

What the major world contemplative and mystical traditions share in common is a thrust toward renewed relationships across the entire spectrum of created being, even to the farthest limits of the universe. All the visionaries of the world's mystical traditions intuit a fundamental source of being that joins all created living things together. The basic principle of this spiritual insight is that the good of one part is the good of all; the diminishment of one is the diminishment of the entire fabric of being. They are one in their understanding that laws operate within the various levels of creation that connect us to each other for the harmonious and orderly functioning of the entire universe. When these laws are not recognized or heeded, the orderly functioning of the universe falls into chaos and all parts of the created reality are affected.

Think of what it would mean to the world and the human family if we each acted and related to one another and to the earth as if our ultimate good depended on the well-being of all other humans and the good of creation. Certainly we would think long and hard about the way we so readily and easily inflict harm and hardship on others in order to advance our own well-being. We would be more cautious about the way we exploit the earth in order to secure our momentary material comfort and security. Insofar as each of us allows our consciousness to be changed, along with our perceptions of our relationships to other persons and to creation, we begin the transformation of our society and our world.

In the Judeo-Christian tradition, God's divine Word is the creative energy from which all being emanates (Gn 1:1–2:25). The original state of innocence was one in which all the various levels of the created universe enjoyed a life-giving unity of peace and blessing in which God "walk[ed] in the garden in the cool of the day" (Gn 3:8). When the fundamental law of unity was broken, alienation—the fragmentation of relationships—was the result. Man and woman experienced shame in their nakedness and covered themselves. God, previously seen as an intimate partner with creation, was now a source of fear and anxiety (Gn 3:10). Creation, a home of peace and well-being for all living things, was now a place of exile and struggle, ultimately leading to death (Gn 3:11-24).

If we look carefully at scriptural revelation, we find that throughout most of our history this fundamental relationship with all things was taken for granted. Our rituals, celebrations, and liturgies reference our relationship with the earth and other living creatures. This relationship has always been a real and vibrant part of our spirituality and worship. Our relationship with God and the authenticity of our worship has been gauged by the strength of our care for the universe and of one another, especially the poor, the needy, and the strangers in our midst. There has been a clear and direct relationship between our life of prayer and faith and the presence and action of God in daily life, manifest through the rhythms and cycles of the created universe. The faith community lived within an unfolding story that wove the disparities and discrepancies of the human condition into a unified fabric of meaning and purpose.

A brief look at our sacramental and liturgical system will remind us that at the very core of our public celebrations is an awareness of the sacred quality of the rhythms of the earth and the significant transitions and passages that mark our journey through life to death. In earlier days especially, crops and farm animals were routinely blessed, the changing of the seasons was marked by feasts with special prayers and processions. Easter is still calculated by the first full moon after the vernal equinox. Christmas, the feast commemorating the coming of light into the world of darkness, comes at the time of the year when the days will begin to get longer.

What this all means is that our spiritual discipline is accessible and functional. It is as close and accessible as the ground we walk on, the place where we work and play. Our Judeo-Christian spirituality is anchored in the rising and setting of the sun, the waxing and waning of the moon. Rain, snow, ice, and hail join with our songs of praise, thanksgiving, and petition to the creator of us all. Our God is present to us in our love-making, our birthing and growing to maturity, our marrying, our being sick, our sinning, and our dying. Christian spirituality is functional. It works. It brings about tangible results in the quality of life and our relationship with the world around us. It affects the quality of the society in which we live and the course of history. While there is an esoteric—that is, internal, mystical—aspect to our faith tradition, there is also a very real and tangible exoteric—external, functional, prophetic—aspect to it. One cannot be separated from the other without adversely affecting the quality of the entire spiritual system.

Right now we are suffering from an over emphasis on the exoteric with a corresponding neglect of the esoteric. Our task now is to bring balance and harmony so that our inner life and outer life function in a mutually life-giving way. We have seen an emphasis on law, ritual, and orthodoxy. As a result we have experienced a decline and neglect of the inner, transformational aspect of religion. We have sought to bring about changes in our lives through reason and the effort of our will. A fully functioning and integrated religious system recognizes and nurtures the interaction and mutually life-giving relationship between external actions and internal transformation. When our actions are not energized by a process of inner transformation, they become wooden, brittle, and ultimately enervating. Ritual and belief become arid, rigid, and dogmatic. Our inner life, disconnected from our external life, may become sentimental and pietistic, resulting in a spirituality that is otherworldly, uninvolved in life's reality. This is evident to us when we see devout persons believing staunchly in their creeds, but who are unmindful of the inconsistencies in their behavior, their callused indifference to the plight of others, their mindless selfish consumption without regard to the poor in our midst or the need of future generations.

Prayer, ceremony, and ritual are essential to our belief system. These aspects however, cannot be separated from the simple and unambiguous acts of reaching out to those in need, caring for the stranger in our midst, forgiving and being forgiven, giving our shirt or coat to the poor, caring for creation. The quality of one aspect affects and determines the quality and authenticity of the other. This discipline of right relationship—especially between inner transformation and external action—is awesomely heroic and difficult. It cuts to the bone and indicts our intense instinct of self-aggrandizement and self-promotion. This spiritual discipline of right relationship can dismantle socio-political, religious, and cultural value systems that sustain and perpetuate our out-of-control consumerism. It can modify our self-absorbed preoccupation with our personal well-being to the exclusion of the well-being of others, and the materialism that dominates our cultural consciousness today and degrades the earth. This dismantling of unenlightened social systems begins with the conversion and transformation of our personal value system. As we allow God access to our inner life to purify and transform us, we begin the transformation of the world in which we live.

In place of the desire for personal and group dominance, our spiritual discipline asks us to place a spirit of love and compassion, honoring all persons equally. In place of self-interest and a spirit of competition, our spiritual discipline asks us to place a spirit of concern for the welfare of all others, extending even to non-human creation. In place of a mindless militarism and materialistic consumerism our spiritual discipline asks us to put our lives and resources on the line in respect for the rights and dignity of others, for the preservation of material creation and non-human life. In place of a drive for personal security, control, and a sense of personal superiority, our discipline asks that we place instead a sense of our universal oneness with all beings in which we recognize that the good of one is the good of all; the diminishment of one is the diminishment and impoverishment of all. This is a very simple and functional way of life but it carries with it the power to transform our world. In contrast, to continue a religious practice that maintains a separation between our inner and outer lives enables us to continue "doing" religion and all its associated practices while allowing our spirituality to remain sentimental, abstract, and theoretical. In the meantime our society and world continue to languish under the ceaseless assault of our unconverted consumerism and our fear-based militarism.

Again, the transformation of consciousness, putting on the mind and heart of Christ, does not begin and end with prayers and rituals, attendance at church, or the orthodoxy of our belief. These are actions that initiate a process of inner transformation leading to a transformation in the way we see and relate to life and the world. Contemplative prayer and a life of contemplative awareness bring about a slow but sure dismantling of the walls of self-interest, allowing our sense of self to reach out and include the entire created universe.

Our prayer and action is a series of cyclic, self-renewing actions; the prayer and rituals are energized and nurtured by our actions, our actions and motivations are nurtured and enriched by our reflective contemplative prayer. In this way contemplative prayer and action form an organic whole, each contributing to the other. Eventually, the separation between prayer and action is dissolved and our life becomes our prayer. Prayer is the totality of our life offered in worship. The public celebrations of worship point to and emanate from our lived experience; the wall of darkness that separates our life from our prayer dissolves and all becomes one. There is no longer the split between contemplation and action, or the choice between contemplation or action; there remains only contemplative action and active contemplation. Our renewed heart center is now the source of a steady flow of loving action with compassion. Our mind and will are taken over by this new flow of energy; our actions, words, and relationships take on a creative spontaneity as social, ego-centric concerns are swept aside in the rush of Christ-centered compassion.

Everything that comes under the rubric of prayer in all its various forms is only the beginning of a long and painful process of dying to our old ego-dominated consciousness. This dying is an opening to an entirely new and expanded consciousness in which we see and understand all creation as an emanation of divine wisdom and self-giving divine love. Our narrow self-interest, our limited and ego-centric understanding of our place in the universe, is replaced by a new awareness that creation is held together by love, and through love all creation, every aspect of it, is drawn back into the life-giving unity from which it came. The Genesis story of creation is more than a story of what once was, it is a story of that which is coming to be through our sacramental action in union with the divine will.

Insofar as you and I place our ego-centric concerns above the love that draws together and unites, we become the dark place in the fabric of creation. Insofar as you and I harbor feelings of hatred, vengeance, or a competitive and adversarial attitude toward others, we are the dark place that prevents the body of Christ from coming to fullness in time. Insofar as we remain indifferent to the plight of the poor and the oppressed, our physical actions and presence in the world cannot be the opening through which the mind and heart of Christ bring peace, compassion, and justice for all. Insofar as greed, lust, and avarice dominate our relationship with the earth, the earth can never again be the nurturing mother that brings forth and sustains life in abundance. Every time we reach out to serve one in need, forgive our enemies, reverence the earth, feed the hungry, and respond with compassion and understanding to those who are marginalized, we become sacraments of Christ's paschal mystery, the agents through which the Kingdom of God is established on earth.

Contemplative living—authentic contemplative prayer—is a process in which we understand and accept the fact that our only reason for being on the earth is to be the means whereby holiness—the holiness of God through Jesus Christ—enters into and remains active and effective through history.

three

Lord, Teach Us to Pray

"Lord, teach us to pray, as John taught his disciples" (Lk 11:1). This longing of the heart expressed by the disciples is an echo of the longing that has resounded within the human heart throughout the ages of our human story. This persistent cry continues to our day and is making itself heard in ever more interesting and insistent ways. This inner imperative to prayer and spiritual practice is reasserting itself in the lives of men and women in all walks of life, even among those who do not consider themselves religious.

The variety of creative expressions is evident in the resurgence of many pagan and neo-pagan rituals, as well as creative innovations that take traditional Christian rituals to new expressions.

I suggest that these innovations are real expressions of the insatiable hunger of the human heart for an experience of a transcendent reality in daily life. This insistent search for religious expression that captures the heart's longing derives from an inner imperative, a law of the heart. If this law of the heart is ignored, the spirit will languish in a deadly sense of incompleteness, an inner poverty that will allow no rest. St. Augustine's often repeated lament comes to mind: "Great art thou O Lord, and greatly to be praised . . . for thou hast formed us for thyself, and we are restless till we find rest in thee" (*Confessions*). This experience that Augustine gives voice to is the experience of the ancient shaman as well as the modern day seeker. To be human is to be conscious; to be conscious is to know and experience our human solitude and our longing to be connected to something larger than ourselves. To be human is to be a restless seeker, a pilgrim of the spirit.

I suggest that this restless spiritual wandering on the part of so many might well serve as a call to reflection and self-examination by the shepherds of our mainstream religions. It is all too easy for those of us who are the designated ministers and priests to become seduced into the complacent comfort of minding the externals of religion and forgetting that ultimately we are charged with transmitting a transformative mystery. We are the designated ministers attending to this universal human longing. We are called to mediate a personal encounter between a living person, Jesus Christ, and those who come seeking him. We neglect this not only to our personal peril, but put at risk the vitality of the churches we serve. We must carry our share of the burden of responsibility for the spiritual famine of our day. The message we carry is for the world, for the earth, not only for the adherents of sectarian creeds. The pastoral task of the church is not to corral people behind dogmatic and ethical fences, but to feed them with the food that nourishes the soul and spirit. When our soul and spirit are nourished and opened to the wellsprings of divine life within, we grow into autonomous and mature carriers and transmitters of faith, grounded in our relationship with the divine.

Many scholars and practitioners of the healing arts have observed that much of our Western cultural disease of the heart and spirit today stems directly from neglect of this inner imperative. There are few informed persons who would deny that we, and our children, are paying a steep price for the neglect of this need for a connection to our inner life of the spirit. I suggest that we will not be able to effect significant changes in the accelerating spiral into violence and self-destruction—our materialism and militaristic posturing—until we see this as symptomatic of our spiritual famine. Our church has its roots deep within the earthy mysticism of our Jewish mothers and fathers. It was incarnate and personified in Jesus Christ, burnished and refined in the deserts of ancient Egypt. Our tradition, together with all the great mystical and contemplative traditions of the world, contains hidden within its liturgical, sacramental and devotional life the key to the creative spiritual energy capable of transforming our world by bringing about dramatic changes from within our heart center.

In Matthew (3:1-12) and Mark (1:1-8), John the Baptist calls for repentance in order to make way for the coming of the kingdom of heaven. He promises a baptism of spirit and fire, certainly images that speak of cleansing and renewal. Luke (3:10-14) is more explicit by demanding that people take a radical stand against the cultural norms that had until then governed human behavior. His demand that the man with two tunics share with the one who has none, and for the tax collector to take no more than his due, are demands that require an inner shift in values and perceptions with a consequent change in behavior that would have seemed quite radical and perhaps even unreasonable to his listeners. It challenged the very means of their livelihood. This is certainly a clear indication that the message of Christ entailed more than the establishment of another temple religion encased in ritual and formulas; Jesus inaugurated a time when true worship engaged the heart of a person and called the believer into a life of service to one's neighbor.

Christ's message was a call to a radical inner transformation that set one against the conventional cultural and religious norms of the day. To be a follower of Christ is to submit oneself to this ongoing inner transformation that leads to freedom from the captivity to one's own selfishness in order to reestablish proper relationships between persons and creation. Jesus—like the prophets before him and all the other great teachers of the world—recognized the futility of attempting to find happiness and rest for the soul until we surrender our will to be aligned with the will of God. "May your will be done on earth as it is in heaven." All the major religious traditions of history in one way or another have attempted to address this universal human longing, a search for a way of life that would establish us in a relationship of harmony with our surroundings.

Today the church transmits the Christ experience to us, and through its prayer life, the celebration of the sacraments, rituals, and devotions, the church empowers us to become sacraments of transformation for our time and place, to be the living signs that transmit this reality to those in our midst. By praying and meditating on the mysteries of the life of Christ through the church, we are awakened to our own deep inner call to live deeply and radically the mystery of Christ's life, passion, death, and resurrection within a community of believers. The transformation of our world begins with the inner transformation of each of us. The church as a community of believers, each one living in a transformative union with God through Christ, becomes a wellspring of transformation for the world.

Through the years as the church has grown and spread across the cultures of the world, it has accumulated a vast array of rituals, practices, and traditions aimed at guiding us into this deep and personal transforming relationship with Christ. Far too many of us, however, have not surrendered ourselves into the deeper mystery, the transforming experience, of our religious life and practice. Many ministers of religion have themselves failed to penetrate the depths of our religious tradition and as a result their ministry to the faithful has remained shallow and unfruitful. In our time many have decided that the church in the past several hundred years had become separated from its inner mystical core, that core that can only be accessed and penetrated through the prayer of the heart that leads to contemplation and an awakening to the mystical vision of Christ. A vision of a new humanity in which the divine image in each of us is brought to perfection.

Today, ministers of religion are hearing the urgent pleas of their parishioners to "teach us to pray." Tragically, all too many ministers of the gospel find themselves ill equipped to respond to this plea. On the other hand, many admit that it is often the example of their parishioners that has prompted them to reexamine their own prayer practices. The number of regular churchgoers who find themselves dissatisfied with a mere routine Sunday service is increasing dramatically. The faithful are realizing that their heart searches for something more, something deeper than mere intellectual belief or conformity to doctrines and rituals joined to a barren routine of church attendance. It is a tribute to the maturity, depth of faith, and honest self-knowledge of many that rather than blame the external structures and practices, they look to their inner self and their personal prayer as a means of bringing new life and vigor to their external practices. Rather than discontinue their Sunday worship or church affiliation, they are seeking ways to deepen their experience by taking up a life of personal prayer and the study of scripture. They are discovering for themselves the hidden depths of the living mystery of Christ alive in the sacraments and the prayer life of our tradition. In this way we are seeing the renewal of our churches from the ground up.

Retreat centers, monasteries, and religious houses note an increasing number of spiritual seekers ready to lay aside the pursuit of the happiness and security offered by the purveyors of secular bliss in order to take significant amounts of time for prayer and personal reflection. Our materialistic society's promise for security and happiness has not only been found wanting, but cruelly seductive. Men and women from all walks of life and belief traditions who actively engage in the tasks of work and raising children somehow find the time and resources to seek out places where they can periodically spend extended periods of time in silence and solitude. Monasteries and religious houses that offer hermitage experiences find their facilities booked months, even a year in advance. Today the ancient call of the prophets for a return to a religion of the heart is coming from within the ranks of the faithful.

All this points to the perennial human search for union with the transcendent; the longing for a grounding in a reality that cannot be swept away by the changing tides and shifting sands of the one-dimensional world of our cultural consciousness. There is a steadily rising tide of people in all walks of life, of all ages and cultural traditions who are realizing that with all our material comfort and technological progress, something fundamental remains elusive and beyond the reach of a materialistic mind. There is a disconnect between our external reality and our inner self-understanding. The reality of our world of material comfort doesn't seem to bring happiness or a deep sense of well being.

The discomfort and pain resulting from this disharmony between our inner and outer life is a catalyst that can motivate us to question and critique the real meaning of our lives and probe beneath the surface of our religious beliefs and practices. The logical question that comes to mind is: If I believe that what I am told is true, if I live as I am told I should, why am I not at peace with my life? This question leads us to plumb beneath the external actions, symbols, and images of our religious beliefs and practices to discover something deeper, a deeper strata of meaning that goes beyond external action to cut to the core and lay open our hearts to be touched, exposed, and judged. On a deep level our life and the motivating forces of our life are seen in a new light, judged by a radical new truth. This is the beginning of a new understanding, a new way of perceiving our lives and our world. We recognize that true religious practice requires that we open our hearts to be emptied and purified of the toxins of our unenlightened cultural value system. Thus emptied and cleansed, we are ready to be filled with the cleansing light of God's will.

Slowly but inexorably, we see the hidden but nonetheless dynamic contemplative and mystical dimension of our religious tradition seep to the surface of our consciousness to penetrate our awareness and move us to take personal responsibility for our spiritual well-being. The spiritual famine of our industrialized society, our excessively rationalized minds, our inflated and ego-driven wills have brought us to an awareness that our hearts and our souls require something more than material, temporal security. Our hearts require more than routine external conformity to institutional and cultural imperatives and mere external conformity to religious laws and rituals.

Students of human behavior and social systems are seeing more clearly how the practice of prayer within a life of faith binds relationships and provides a stable ground for our social institutions. The other side of this coin reveals that the absence of prayer and faith often cause spiritual distress that leads to unhealthy relationships and a weakening of our social institutions.

We are discovering in ever greater numbers that our Christian tradition all along has been the carrier, the container of spiritual truths and dimly perceived realities for which our hearts have been longing. The unacknowledged truths contained in this forgotten wisdom are the missing components of a sound and healthy life in a world ever shifting and moving beneath our feet.

Our present day spiritual thirst has opened the eyes and sensitized the hearts of many to see that our sacraments, liturgical practices, and sacred scriptures—as well as our traditional devotions—are not ends in themselves, magic rituals bringing instant if superficial contentment. Rather they are doorways through which we pass to embrace a personal encounter and ultimate union with our God. We see and understand that our restless, unrequited anxieties, our alienated drifting into barren relationships, our endless pursuit of material goods, our fear-based militarism, are manifestations of our innate spiritual hunger for the God we profess to believe in. They are false gods offering cheap bliss and fleeting security. The pain of our society is the pain of having failed to believe that Jesus' promise that we are called to live our lives in a real, experiential union of love with God, expressed in love of neighbor, is real and meant for us in the concrete historical reality of our human lives with one another in our work-a-day world.

When the disciples asked Jesus, "Lord, teach us to pray," Jesus responded by teaching them a formula of prayer to the Father that gave expression to a vision of a new order, a new creation in which the will of God and will of human beings were united. The Lord's

Prayer envisions a creation in which human hearts are joined together under the light of divine wisdom. It is a vision of humanity liberated from those forces that divide and fragment the human family into adversarial and competitive camps, each vying for dominance and control over the other. The Lord's Prayer is a formula expressing a belief in the possibility of a new way of living on earth in Christlike relationships with one another and the earth. It articulates a bold and daring vision of a world in which God, humanity, and creation are bound together in mutually life-giving and sustaining love.

This prayer formulates a radical and revolutionary vision of human possibility that is at the same time an uncompromising indictment of our unenlightened conventional value system of ruthless competition, unbridled consumerism, militarism and the predatory use of power and might to establish a reign of the powerful over the weak and powerless. It is a formula for a new consciousness, a consciousness that sees the unity of all creation bound together in the life of the one God, *Abba*, Father, the source of all that exists. But as Father, God is the one who continually embraces creation within a womb of compassion, the one to whom we may confidently surrender our life. The life of each one of us bonded in compassion and love to one another gives flesh and concrete action here and now to God's compassionate, caring presence. In other words your life and mine are the continuation of the life of Jesus Christ through time. This is the meaning of "Blessed are the poor in spirit, theirs is the Kingdom of Heaven." To truly know God as *Abba* is to know God in whose loving embrace all creation rests, to know and rest in the one in whom we have our very being. To be poor in spirit means that nothing else is necessary. Under the watchful care of *Abba*, as true children of the one Father, we incorporate into our lives and actions the same care for one another and creation that our Father in heaven has for us.

This prayer telescopes the totality of Christ's proclamation of the reign of God in the hearts of humankind into a few brief words. As such, it is a prayer, if attended to on more than a routine and superficial level, that seeks to penetrate the heart and bring to fruition the seeds of our longing for a life in a world where the sacredness of our immediate relationship to God is paramount and the sacredness of every human person and all creation is the ruling value that guides our life on earth. It is a prayer that holds out the promise of elevating the human person to the dignity of a co-creator with God and a co-redeemer with Jesus in bringing about a kingdom of peace and justice here on earth.

Each of us in our own way experiences the perennial longing of the heart which gave rise to the disciples' plea: "Lord, teach us to pray as John taught his disciples." Beneath this longing, if we attend to it, prayer, contemplative prayer, and a mystical consciousness await birth into our life and action. This new life of intimacy with God is available to us beneath the surface of our commonly accessible daily devotions that have been a part of our religious tradition for centuries. For our heart's desire for this deep, transforming grace to be realized, prayer must be accompanied by a living faith and trust that it is possible for anyone to grow into a contemplative union with God. For this to happen we must divest ourselves of our cultural conditioning that tells us that the higher states of contemplative and mystical union with God are reserved for the few and the special. Jesus taught no such doctrine of exclusivity. He addressed directly the human heart's openness and longing for this union and vigorously chided those who would have taught otherwise. We have to approach our prayer, as simple and as basic as that might be, with the confident trust that God created us just for such union and in fact requires this kind of intimacy for the work of redemption to be continued and brought to fruition in the world.

Another cultural deception that has to be overcome is the notion that only the non-Christian religious traditions teach and practice the contemplative way of life, that if one wants to develop a contemplative consciousness, one must embrace meditative practices peculiar to those belief systems. Indeed, many Catholics and other Christians have studied and practiced these disciplines with great benefit. However, many, like myself, after delving into these practices, have discovered that they pointed us back in the direction of our own tradition with a renewed belief and confidence in the efficacy of our cherished traditional practices.

The Christian tradition is eminently grounded in an active and engaged life in the work-a-day world of toil and play. The practices and devotions of the Christian church lend themselves to an active and engaged life with family and society. They provide the means of creating an inner spiritual environment that enables one to be present to the demands of the world while maintaining a new perspective grounded in the values of the gospel.

I believe strongly that our world has arrived at a time when only this strong and irresistible force of love poured forth from the hearts and lives of our faith community will turn the tide of history toward the establishment of a world where peace and justice with compassion replaces the storm of violence and vengeance which is common today. I believe further that the faith communities that will transform our society and world will not be those faith communities known for their adherence to specific doctrines and creeds which tend to separate us into adversarial camps; rather the faith communities that will unleash a new fire on the earth will be gathered in the prayer that opens their hearts to be cleansed and filled with the radical message of God's living Word.

Hearts and lives are not changed by theology or law. The church that proclaims the message of Jesus Christ is the church that must jettison all pretenses of power and control, exclusivity and superiority, to become a church that is a gathering of persons profoundly steeped in and purified by the cleansing fire of God's living Word. This is the same Word that brought creation into being and lifted Moses from the status of a murderer and fugitive to a leader filled with the power of God. This is the Word that disrupted the life of the prophets and finally became fully incarnate in Jesus Christ. The Word incarnate in Jesus filled the heart of Herod with terror, amazed and frightened the shepherds. Peter was filled with fear when Jesus called him to discipleship. The apostles and disciples of Jesus were led to the cross where their dreams and hopes were crucified. No wonder then that the coming of the Word of God into our life brings consternation and dismay. It threatens to wreck and destroy our carefully constructed realities. Out of this wreckage a new fire is released upon the earth. The apostles and disciples found their lives filled with a new power, a clarified vision of what life could be. Possessed by this fire, they went forth into the world and even in their suffering, failures and ultimate death by martyrdom, they conquered the world. That fire remains faintly smoldering within the hearts of each of us baptized into Christ. Our subtle, haunting dissatisfaction breathes life into the embers of that divine fire within. Our contemplative openness to the Word ignites the embers to become a fire on the earth. If there is reason to be afraid of the fire, there is more reason to fear the dead coals of a fire extinguished.

four

The Holy Spirit and Contemplative Prayer

Pentecost is the birthday of the church; it commemorates the event in which the Spirit of the risen Lord was poured out not only on the community of the faithful, but all creation as well. Pentecost is our creation story. It marks the emergence of a new humanity and a new creation from the old. Recall how the disciples had to be cleansed from their hopes, dreams, and expectations. After the crucifixion, they were a disillusioned and defeated group. They were locked in fear in the upper room not knowing what to do or expect. A hard but necessary lesson to learn is that to follow Christ to the resurrection is to follow him to the abandonment and darkness of the cross. This is more than poetic imagery. It is the story of our soul moving toward union with the divine. It is a movement from darkness to light.

Unlike the first creation story where humans followed non-human creation, this creation story posits a new humanity, equipped with a new consciousness, as the foundation of the new creation. In the old creation story humanity was created from the earth and infused with the breath of God. In this new creation story, a new creation emerges from a new humanity. Material creation will be enwrapped in human flesh, fired and forged by divine love now enfleshed in persons.

In the gospel of John there is a dramatic and significant episode that takes place after the resurrection (Jn 20:21-23). Jesus appears to his disciples and offers them his peace. Then in a significant gesture, but one that is consistent with the overall theme of his gospel, Jesus breathes on his disciples, then tells them to receive the Holy Spirit. But the reception of the Holy Spirit comes with the command to forgive one another's sins.

In Genesis, God breathed into the stuff of the earth and earth became conscious in human flesh. Now Jesus, the Word of God, the Word through whom creation came into being, breathes on the community of followers and they become the soil out of which a new humanity arises. In Genesis humankind was commanded to multiply and fill the earth. In the Christian covenant the new humanity begins with the command to forgive sins, to mend the broken fabric of human relationships.

The church without pentecost, without the breath of the Spirit guiding us, is like a fully rigged sailing ship without the wind. The body of the faithful through their life of prayer and union with the risen Christ gives flesh, presence, and action to the Holy Spirit in the church. Similarly, our individual life of prayer, ritual, and orthodoxy of belief without the animating breath of the Holy Spirit is like a body without breath. Yes, we need to be reminded that it is possible for us to go through the actions of religious practice while remaining deaf to the inspirations of the Holy Spirit. "Today, if you hear his voice, do not harden your hearts . . ." (Heb 4:7). Prayer is the action of our heart that gives the Spirit space to be present in our lives and through our lives, in the church, and through the church, in the world. Our life of faith, our rituals and celebrations, our belief in doctrines, without the movement of the Holy Spirit fully praying and acting in union with our spirit, is like a ship be-calmed. Therefore I want to repeat what I have said before. The rituals, forms, and actions we perform under the rubric of "prayer" are only the external shell that provide structure and focus for an inner, very personal and subjective experience of God within us. The externals of what we call prayer are meant to lead us to an engagement with God's Spirit praying within us unceasingly. In this engagement our spirit and the divine Spirit are one in prayer. All our prayer, and ultimately everything we do, is absorbed into, and becomes one with, the prayer of the Holy Spirit. Our life, our action becomes the prayer of God's own Spirit. And all becomes one with the eternal priestly prayer of Jesus Christ being offered for the healing and redemption of humankind and all creation. In Jesus there was no separation between his actions, his prayer, and his life in union with the Father's will. All of this was manifest and made real in his heroic act of forgiveness from the cross.

Pentecost marks the event in which the power of Christ was imparted to the community of disciples to fill them with the boldness, the courage, and the freedom to move beyond the locked doors of their fear and timidity to go forth into the world and preach the gospel to all creation. The Holy Spirit inspired more than mere words and ideas. The entire person was possessed by a new vision, a new way of seeing things and responding to their world. The church, in the lives of the faithful, was now the arena in which the action of the Holy Spirit was being realized. The young church had been captured, emptied of all personal concerns and preoccupations and filled with the mind of Christ. The minds of the faithful, previously enshrouded in darkness, were now opened to the full realization of the meaning of the life, word, and action of Jesus. The mind of Christ was now their mind also. Now they saw the true reality beyond the veils of their previously clouded perceptions. They were living in the world, but the horizons of their understanding had been opened to include the total reality that transcended all time and space. The veils that separated time from eternity had been pierced.

First and foremost it is important to remember that it was individual persons who opened themselves to the Holy Spirit and through whom the Holy Spirit penetrated and empowered the church. It was individual persons whose minds had been opened by the piercing fire of God's Word. Now they understood that the words and actions of Jesus contained the force of the divine Word that was the Word behind the order and truth of creation. It is here that we encounter the intimate relationship between the Word of God and the Holy Spirit. It is necessary to spend some time reflecting on the Word of God and its energizing movement in our inner life, for it is the Word of God that is the medium by which the Holy Spirit gains access to our lives.

In the imagery of St. Luke, the young church and the disciples considered themselves to be ministers of the Word (Lk 1:2). Their entire life was subservient to the power of the Word. Nothing stood between them and their response to the movement of the Word in their life. The word "minister" here refers to being subject to or inferior to someone or something, a sense of being under or beneath. In the sense in which Luke is using the word, the disciple is the servant of the Word, at the disposal of the power of the Word. We need to take a moment to reflect on the deeper meaning of this notion. Unless we understand the inner meaning of the way in which the Word possessed and transformed the heart, mind, and consciousness of the first apostles and disciples, we can fall into the trap of thinking that the Word is ours to use as an instrument to serve our limited mind and will. Or worse yet, we can imagine that the living Word of God is just another idea rattling around in our heads, void of energy and vitality. We forget that the Word we are contemplating is the same living utterance that was sent forth into the darkness and chaos to bring forth harmony, light, and order. Jesus is the same Word now incarnate in human flesh; the Word of power, of new life, of order and harmony that now wants to take possession of our flesh to continue bringing order from chaos, life to the void.

The authority of the gospel and the name of Jesus are often invoked in our time to shore up the opinions and pet values of the one who thinks he or she is speaking in God's name. This is just as true of some church officials as it is of the lay person. As often as not the Word is used to reinforce social, economic, political, and religious agendas of individual politicians and teachers. The Word of God is as often as not used to affirm and validate darkness as light, chaos as the desired order of things. Lies and deceptions are as often as not cloaked within "God's word." Mediocre and tepid religion often masquerades as God's Word.

Again we must refer back to the seminal experiences of the early church. The first disciples of the Word, Jesus' immediate followers, were prepared for pentecost by a radical, and one might say, ruthless, stripping away of their old consciousness. Their stripping and cleansing was every bit as uncompromising as was the crucifixion and death of Jesus himself. They had to be totally emptied of everything they believed in and hoped for. Only then could they receive and embrace something that was totally new, totally beyond their previous ability to grasp and take to themselves. They were emptied and cleansed in order that they might become carriers of a message that was totally beyond the ability of their conventional mind to conceive.

The message we receive and carry today is every bit as confounding as was theirs. In fact it is the same stumbling block for human logic as it has always been. This explains why it is so often reduced to the narrow horizons of human logic. Christianity becomes just another human organization to which we pay our nominal dues of perfunctory church attendance, but which requires no substantial or significant change in behavior or values.

This radical surrender to the Word of God is reminiscent of Mary's prayer at the annunciation: "I am the Lord's servant. . . . May it be to me as you have said" (Lk 1:38). We are taken and possessed by a new life, a life that can open up unimagined new depths of human potential. Like Mary, possessed by this new life, we are taken to places where we would never choose to go, to do that which we could never choose to do.

This notion captures fully the contemplative stance of the Christian and the church as a body. This notion might perhaps be closest to the truest, most pure meaning of what it means to be a contemplative. A contemplative person is truly a minister—a servant—in that the heart and soul have been completely taken over by the mind of Christ through contemplation of the Word.

Contemplation in the marian sense means to be open to be impregnated by the Word, to allow the Word to become flesh in our flesh. According to this understanding a minister must be first and foremost a contemplative, one whose life is spent in quiet, humble contemplation of the Word. One's life is completely blended with the mystery of Christ. The union results in the Christ event completely filling up the person's mind, will and heart, taking possession of one's actions; in short, being flesh in us. Coming at this notion from the other direction we can conclude that a contemplative person, that is, one in whom the Word is the active force behind his or her life, is therefore a minister—a servant. From this we recognize that many officially "ordained" ministers who function in the name of the church are not genuine "ministers," while many of those not officially "ordained" are nonetheless true ministers of the Word.

We are dealing here with a sensitive and delicate interaction between our understanding of the Word of God and the Spirit of God poured out upon humanity and all the earth. It is the Word of God that prepares us to be temples of God's living Spirit. The Word comes into our darkness, our brokenness, to reveal to us what we are called to be. The Word reveals the truth of creation and more especially the inner truth of each person created in God's image. When we allow ourselves to be led by the Word into the truth of our personhood, we enter into a process of cleansing and renewing. Jesus, as the Word incarnate, led the apostles and first followers to the death to self that allowed space for the Holy Spirit at Pentecost.

The second reading for Pentecost is taken from the first letter of Paul to the Corinthians. It reads: "no one can say 'Jesus is Lord,' except by the Holy Spirit" (1 Cor 12:3). This passage requires us to look deeper into our life of prayer and devotion. "Jesus is Lord" can be said on a variety of levels. In the context in which Paul is speaking he is obviously referring to an action, an inner act of surrender to the Spirit within.

It is obvious that no one can make such a radical surrender of their entire life and action to God on a merely superficial level. The words must spring from an inner event, an awakening to new realities that allows one to see beyond the surface. It is the inner event that is of the essence, that gives reality to the words. If the inner event is not present, the words are merely sounds with no substance. To accept the truth of the Word as the truth of our life is to enter into a relationship that prepares us for this inner event; the freedom and the light to see and proclaim Jesus as Lord.

It is also well to remember that it is possible to bring about inner events through the repetition of words or phrases. Thus, the words of Mary's prayer of surrender at the Annunciation, repeated mindfully and with heartfelt devotion, will bring about changes in one's inner life. In a similar fashion, the Jesus prayer, repeated over and over again for a significant period of time, will bring about a mind and heart molded on the mind and heart of Jesus Christ. So, really, prayer is a cooperative interaction or dialogue between our action, our words, and that of the Holy Spirit. What is essential to remember is that the words and images of our prayer must represent an inner willingness to be led, taught, and purified. Drawing this idea out a bit further, we can now see why the celebration of the liturgy, the repetition of the formal prayers of the church, done mindfully, with hearts open to receive the inner mystery of these actions, can lead to a change of heart, a conversion.

To say "Jesus is Lord" and mean it with all its ramifications means to surrender one's life to be transformed entirely through the paschal mystery of the life, passion, death, and resurrection of Jesus. This is not possible to do without the aid of the Holy Spirit. It requires that the mind and heart be opened to an entirely new vision of reality and an awareness of what is possible for the human person. It is the pearl of great price that enables one to sell everything in order to purchase the pearl. But first it is a matter of having the vision to recognize the pearl. This is the inner knowledge that enables one to abandon everything, all attachments and illusions, and set off on a new path. Many of us in the church live in the midst of an abundance of pearls, but lack the vision to recognize them. Or we have lost the ability to discern real pearls from the false ones.

The words "Jesus is Lord" are the surface expression of a dramatic inner shift in perceptions, a shift that will change the course of one's life in all aspects. Something new has pierced the veils of illusions and opened the eyes of the heart to the full meaning and understanding of the Incarnation of God in Jesus. It is the person pierced and opened by the Word who can utter this prayer of radical enlightenment and surrender to union with God's Holy Spirit. Once the heart has been pierced at this level, the words of the prayer are no longer mere words repeated, but rather they spring from the very wellspring of the heart, they express an inner event, an event that unites the person's prayer to the eternal prayer of the heart of Christ, and therefore to the heart of every living human being. One's prayer then becomes the expression of the as yet unrealized, unacknowledged prayer of our universal human longing for union with God, even the unrecognized and unacknowledged longing of the most hardened sinner.

Perhaps the full and radical meaning of this passage is fully captured for us in Thomas's act of faith in the risen Lord, "My Lord and my God!" (Jn 20:28). Or again when Jesus asked his disciples, "who do people say the Son of Man is?" and Peter responded, "You are the Christ, the Son of the living God" (Mt 16:13-16). These statements obviously come from some deep inner knowledge that opens the hearts of Thomas and Peter to see beyond the surface to inner realities. They recognize the mystery of God acting in Jesus, while others see merely another preacher and wonder worker. The words they utter have their source in the Holy Spirit now alive and active in their lives. Their subsequent lives of service to the Word—and death by martyrdom—drew out the full meaning of these statements.

Early in this first letter to the Corinthians Paul speaks of his abandonment of, and turning away from, the power and influence of the false wisdom of the world. He rejects the "wise and persuasive words" of the worldly wise, that is, the ones still enshrouded in the illusory wisdom of an unenlightened world (1 Cor 2:4). He speaks of a wisdom of the mature, but not the wisdom of this age (v. 6).

> No, we speak of God's secret wisdom, a wisdom that has been hidden and that God destined for our glory before time began. None of the rulers of this age understood it, for if they had, they would not have crucified the Lord of glory. . . . No eye has seen, no ear has heard, no mind has conceived what God has prepared for those who love him but God has revealed it to us by his Spirit (1 Cor 2:7-10).

Thomas and Peter, indeed any who truly say "Jesus is Lord" are speaking from this same wisdom that has been hidden from the beginning of time and is now being realized in Jesus Christ for the glory of all.

This is the prayer of the Holy Spirit that waits to be liberated and given expression in our life of prayer. Prayer is the foremost action of the Holy Spirit in our lives. Under the influence of the Holy Spirit, our prayer is a process of opening our minds and hearts to God. Prayer is an action, any action or discipline, that opens our minds and hearts to God. It allows God, through the Holy Spirit, to enter into and take possession of our lives from the center where new life radiates outward into our life of action and relationship. It allows our minds to be one with the mind of Christ in such a way that the petition of the Lord's Prayer is realized in our life, "Father, may your name be made holy, may your

Kingdom come, may your will be done on earth as it is in Heaven. . . ." The person becomes the center for the action of the Holy Spirit on earth. God's will is done on earth through the union of our will with the will of God just as it was in Jesus. Our life becomes the sacrament of God's presence on earth just as it was in the life of Jesus.

This is the goal of the church on earth; the realization of a body of believers who not only believe with their minds, but whose very lives and all their thoughts and actions are brought into conformity with the mind and heart of Christ.

St. Paul offers a startling revelation of our true relationship with God in the Holy Spirit if we would allow the truth of his words to enter into our heart. It requires some serious reflection and then a radical act of faith to surrender to the mystery contained in Paul's words. He states in 1 Corinthians 2:10-16, that the Spirit of God that searches all and knows the inner mystery of God is the same Spirit that has been given to us. In other words, the inner wisdom and truth of God that the Spirit knows is now resident within us. In verse 16 Paul asks: "But who knows the mind of the Lord that he may instruct Him?" He then adds triumphantly, "But we have the mind of Christ." Yes we have nested within the deep inner recesses of our soul the very wisdom and truth of the divine by the presence of the Holy Spirit within us, the Holy Spirit that knows the mind of God.

Buried beneath the debris of our culturally conditioned ego-mind, we have the Spirit of God waiting for our invitation to emerge into our consciousness, renewing and transforming our minds and thoughts into those of Christ so that Christ lives in us. "May your Kingdom come, your will be done on earth as it is in heaven." The full ripening of the fruits of this prayer in the hearts of the faithful brings about a very concrete and material transformation of the earth. "Thy Kingdom come, thy Will be done on earth as it is in heaven," is the realization of the human person, transformed by the fire of divine love within the heart so that each person in the believing Christian community is in fact a fully realized Christic person, a zone of unqualified love for all other human and non-human creation. Love is contagious; as love flows out from the center of each person, love becomes the energizing force of evolution and the directing force of history.

This is the goal and fruit of a life of contemplation. Contemplative prayer is the prayer that matures our faith and deepens it from one-dimensional, external rituals and devotions to a personal inner union with the divine. In humble, patient, and persevering openness to God's Word in sacred scripture, the teachings and traditions of the church, the community of faithful people, and the work of creation, we slowly but surely peel away the sheaths of self-interest and the egocentricity of our lives. We gradually liberate our mind from the unredeemed, unenlightened cultural toxins that enslave us to reveal hidden deep within the heart center the pure light of God's holy wisdom. Our conscious mind is now open to be led, taught, purified, and guided in our actions. "I have been crucified with Christ, and I no longer live, but Christ lives in me" (Gal 2:20). This is the fruition of our baptismal immersion into Christ who is now coming to maturity in our lives and action. The church is the temple of the living God, but we are the living stones of the temple, each in our own way being transformed, re-formed into the mind of Christ. The kingdom comes alive in each one of us; God's will is done on earth as it is in heaven in our lives of contemplative awareness and redemptive action.

Think now about how this affects our understanding of the "second coming of Christ." Try to grasp the notion, with the consequent awesome responsibility, that this cosmic event is to begin within the depths of our God-like self, our true self awakened and actualized in God-like relationships with one another and all creation. It is the full perfection of the image of God within each of us. In short I suggest that the second coming of Christ breaks forth from within the heart of each of us. Perhaps Paul is intuiting this, hoping for this when he prays in the letter to the Ephesians.

> For this reason I kneel before the Father, from whom his whole family in heaven and on earth derives its name. I pray that out of his glorious riches he may strengthen you with power through his Spirit in your inner being, so that Christ may dwell in your hearts through faith. And I pray that you, being rooted and established in love, may have power, together with all the saints, to grasp how wide and long and high and deep is the love of Christ, and to know this love that surpasses knowledge—**that you may be filled to the measure of all the fullness of God** (Eph 3:14-19, *my emphasis*).

five

Cultivating the Heart Center

We have seen that the foundation of all our prayer and devotion is God's eternal Word revealed through Jesus Christ. The church mediates this Word of revelation through the liturgy, scripture and the living tradition of the faith community. But God's Word is also being revealed to us in creation, the daily events of our lives and the unfolding historical events of our time in history. There is no place, no event, no circumstance that is not a moment of divine revelation. The ground of all contemplative prayer and mindful living is life itself in all its varied aspects. The goal of any spiritual discipline is to awaken our slumbering hearts to be sensitive and responsive to God's presence in life.

All life is a sacred reading, a *lectio divina,* all action is a response to God's sovereignty over creation. In the contemplative Christian, God's kingdom is to be established in the hearts of all now, God's will is to be done on earth as it is in heaven here now. The human will is created to be the sacrament by which divine truth is accomplished on earth as it is in heaven. Ultimately Jesus Christ is available to us immediately and personally through the Holy Spirit living within each of us through the community of faith. Therefore all scripture reading, *lectio,* personal prayer, celebration of the mysteries of faith in the liturgy, the sacraments, and whatever other devotions we might practice, are aimed at leading us to this personal and intimate union with Jesus Christ now present in the church through the Holy Spirit. Consider St. Paul's words to the Corinthians:

> The Spirit searches all things, even the deep things of God. For who among men knows the thoughts of a man except the man's spirit within him? In the same way no one knows the thoughts of God except the Spirit of God. We have not received the spirit of the world but the Spirit who is from God, that we may understand what God has freely given us (1 Cor 2:10-12).

Here is an extraordinary teaching about our relationship to the Holy Spirit and our immediate access to the Wisdom of God in the depths of our being. The Spirit that knows the inner life of God has been given to us. Through that Spirit dwelling within us we are now able to put on the mind of Christ. Our actions, thoughts, and perceptions—indeed our very self-identities—are now entirely transformed into a sacrament of God. Through the Spirit of God living within us the actions of our lives have the potential to make present the light and truth of divine wisdom.

However, for this to happen, we ourselves need to be cleansed and purified from everything in our lives that is contrary to the divine will. As long as our cultural ego dominates our actions, as long as our primary concern in life is our own narrow self-interest, the Wisdom and light of God is locked away in our hearts under the debris of our unrecognized and unacknowledged sinfulness.

The church itself has as a single mission, the encounter of each baptized person with the risen Christ. This encounter is not intended to remain on a theoretical, theological level only, but is experiential and heart-felt, a knowing God in our deep inner self. This knowing is akin to the knowing that God has for each of us within God's own inner life. It is the knowing of lovers in which each becomes a part of the other's inner self-knowing. This personal encounter is always within the context of our lived experience.

After the revelation of creation itself, sacred scripture is the most ancient story of the actions of God in history remembered and passed on to us by the ancient community of faith. I believe it is accurate to say that the revelation of creation and the revelation contained in our sacred scriptures are in fact one continuous revelation. In Genesis we read that God "spoke" a word and creation came into being. The imagery here suggests that the word of God speaks forth the inner truth of God, heretofore held within the inner mystery of God, but now revealed in creation. Creation is the unfolding self-revelation of God. Humanity, each person, is essentially a unique bringing forth of the inner mystery of God.

Jesus' life and action as the Word of God incarnate in human flesh does not reveal an abstract truth, a new philosophy, but rather a very concrete and practical way to know God. Jesus reveals the perfect, unblemished truth of the human person as an image of the divine. To see and understand Jesus is to see and grasp the lost, forgotten truth of ourselves in which the image of God is found in its perfection. To follow the teachings of Jesus is to embark on a path that will lead us to our true selves and establish us in a life of harmony, of oneness with ourselves as well as with human and non-human creation. Jesus' words and miracles reveal a person whose life was in perfect accord with the life-giving and nurturing powers of creation.

The Word of God in sacred scripture is our most immediate and personal means of encountering God's will for us as we seek to understand it in the daily events and challenges we meet each day. By daily conforming our lives to the Wisdom of God revealed in sacred scripture, we gradually move away from the false values of the world into a more life-giving harmony with the deep and hidden mystery of what it means to be human, created in the divine image and therefore at one with the truth of our world.

For those of us in the Judeo-Christian tradition, the Word of God is the bedrock of our spiritual path to union with God. For the baptized Christian, Jesus Christ is the fulfillment of the entire history of God present in powerful action in the community of believers. Jesus is the Word of God made flesh, now living through history in the servant community. Christian scriptures make his Word and action present to us through time. Our contemplative, prayerful openness allows God's Word to take flesh in our lives. The life of Jesus continues through history in our flesh. As we interiorize the Word of God, and the images and symbols of our faith, our very being and action in the world becomes prayer, the prayer of the Holy Spirit.

During the course of Christian history other effective methods of meditating on the mystery of the life of Jesus were developed as a means of aiding people in the search to live in union with Christ. It is well for us to remember that personal union with Christ is a transformative union and has always been the expected fruit of all prayer, devotion, and celebration in the church. The full fruit of this transformative prayer has been the experience of those who bring an attitude of openness and receptivity. If our mind is closed around rigid expectations, egocentric hopes, an attitude of control, our prayer is likely to remain on a very surface level. While this transformative and healing union with Christ is slow and gradual over many years of dedicated and patient practice, it results in a renewed and transformed spirit that radically changes a person's way of being and acting in the world. It is a change that emerges from the inner depths of the person resulting in a new creation, a new way of being a human being.

Opening the mind and heart to God is the most fundamental movement toward a life of prayer in which God in the Holy Spirit becomes the living force of all our thoughts and actions. While this seems a simple and straightforward principle, it requires patience and perseverance in a discipline that stands in contradiction to our cultural conditioning. Real prayer is countercultural. It challenges our usual conventional mind set and cultural expectations. To take a life of prayer seriously is an act of judgment, an indictment of the unenlightened cultural values of our time and place in history. A person of prayer makes a dramatic and unambiguous statement that the manic, self-indulgent values of our cultural environment no longer dominate one's life and action.

One of the most common obstacles to the deepening of our prayer is the stubborn and seemingly intractable "busyness" of the ego-mind. Our inner life seems to be hopelessly captivated by our unending stream of thoughts, images, fantasies, and memories that immediately surge to the surface of our consciousness as soon as we attempt to lay aside our tasks and attempt to settle into prayer. Sometimes this inner material is accompanied by distressing and disturbing feelings that nag at our conscience and rob us of the peace and consolation we seek in prayer. The way many, if not most of us, cope with this inner activity is to attempt to keep ourselves busy, engaged in mental activity that allows us to screen out this unwanted material. Busy, wordy prayer, or a prayer that is characterized by a fretful or anxious state of mind, while well-intended, can be an obstacle to a deeper interior prayer that leads to a conscious union with God. This prayer is being dominated by a mindset of control; a mindset that expects specific results and expects and hopes that God will conform to one's will.

This tactic prevents our prayer from moving beneath rational, intellectual, and volitional activity. It was mentioned above that the human mind and will alone are not capable of penetrating into the eternal mystery of God and our personal deep inner life. We need to find a way to move beyond this obstacle to plumb the depths of our deep hidden inner self where the Spirit of God dwells. It is from this deep inner space that God's Spirit will reveal to us the hidden truth of God's Word that at the same time reveals our own hidden truth. It is only when our mind is freed from its intellectual boundaries and joined to our intuitive and affective functions that true knowledge emerges into consciousness; our mind becomes whole, open to knowledge not available to intellect alone. Our intellectual knowledge is enriched and deepened, burnished by inner intuitive knowledge. The fruit of this inner knowledge joined to intellectual knowledge is a creative spontaneity, an innovative and adventurous—even a playful—way of engaging in the conundrums and dilemmas of our daily lives. Allowing the ego to remain dominant in our prayer leads to the sad circumstance in which many of us pray only on the very thin upper crust of an experience of the deep mystery of faith nested within our biblical heritage as well as within our neglected inner self.

I pointed out earlier that divine revelation not only reveals to us the hidden mystery of the divine, but it also reveals to us the forgotten truth of our human nobility. It reveals to us the source of the longings of our heart. To remain on the thin upper crust of prayer denies us the wisdom and compassion that comes from a deeper self-knowledge.

The result of this truncated journey of prayer is that we remain limited in our understanding of the Word of God in our lives and are locked into a shallow and fragmented understanding of our own true selves and our place in the scheme of redemption. Prayer then becomes an attempt to coerce and manipulate God's will to fit our narrow perceptions. We reduce God's infinite wisdom to the dimensions of our limited understanding. The fruit of a deeper and more authentic prayer moves us in the other direction. It opens us to allow our understanding to be enlarged, joined to the will of God. Our will and understanding of things and events are drawn into the infinite and eternal wisdom of God, the wisdom that transcends natural human understanding. We move from hoping and desiring that God will make things turn out according to our will to an attitude of surrender into the larger mystery of God's understanding.

It was in darkness and an experience of failure and abandonment that Jesus surrendered in obedience to the Father's inscrutable will on Calvary and was received from that abandonment into the eternal embrace of the Father. The lesson for us is that in spite of all evidence to the contrary, God's almighty will and sovereignty rule, and God does not abandon us. In times of darkness and seeming abandonment, it is for us to wait in patience and trust, knowing that divine wisdom will be revealed in its own good time. It is God's will that each of us live in this complete and loving trust in the Father's love and fidelity. It is God's will that we be drawn up, our mind and consciousness opened and enlarged to an understanding and acceptance of the inscrutable mystery of God's will and plan for our life.

The central truth of the Incarnation of God in Jesus Christ is to remind us that our true purpose in creation is to enjoy a personal and unmediated union with the Triune God of all creation, the source and end of all. Jesus, as the perfect revelation of the inner mystery of God, who contains and reveals the mystery of the universe, is also at the same time the perfect and final revelation of each human person. He is the revelation of the person restored to right order with God and the created universe. Jesus was speaking out of his own relationship with God when he sought to teach the apostles and disciples to pray: "May your name be made holy, may your Kingdom come, your will be done on earth as it is in Heaven. . . ."

Jesus, as the true revelation of creation and each human person, knew and honored the God-life dormant within each person. His radical, and to some scandalous, inclusion of sinners and the socially and religiously outcast into his circle of friends stands as a statement of his recognition of the value and nobility of each person no matter what the external appearances might be. It is an unambiguous indictment of our social and religious divisions. What is most important for us to see is that this radical inclusiveness of Jesus is a revelation of our latent but nonetheless real and urgent quest for a "Holy Communion" with all our sisters and brothers as well as non-human creation. Jesus reveals to us something about ourselves that we didn't know, something hidden beneath the surface of our ego defenses. Beneath the ego-inspired, fear-based divisions of our lives, we long for unity. Contemplation leads us into our fearful inner darkness to the empty space within each of us that can only be filled by the

God who is the ground of the life of all our sisters and brothers. Jesus leads us to the indwelling God by insisting on an unconditional reconciliation with the most abandoned, the most misunderstood and unloved of our sisters and brothers. Contemplative prayer is first and foremost a path leading to this radical union with God by opening us to an awareness of our radical union with the entire human family and with non-human creation as well.

Jesus models for us that absolute faith that enables us to live in unshakeable trust even in moments of seeming abandonment and the darkness of our limited senses. This abandonment and living faith is not accessible through rational analysis and strength of will; it is the fruit of a heart and mind transformed by a new, experiential knowledge of God in and with us. It is the fruit of contemplative prayer. It is the knowledge that can only come from experience.

It is only the Divine Word, that perfect image of God in human flesh, that can reveal who we really are, created in the divine image. The Word entering into our hidden self shines on and reveals the inner secret of our true self known only to God. When we awaken to who we really are, grounded in the life of God, knowing that God's life is the life of our existence, then we live our lives rooted in the bedrock that can never be shaken or taken away. All of our actions and experiences, all events and circumstances of our lives are perceived and understood from the perspective of this inner experiential knowledge. This is the hidden treasure lying beneath our cluttered and fragmented minds, the treasure that lies at the end of our contemplative journey.

It seems clear then that growth in contemplative prayer requires a radical alteration of the way in which we understand and deal with the inner clutter that maintains our prayer and our inner life as two separate realities. Our growth in prayer and in our relationship with God depends on the way in which we respond to the obstacles that stand between us and in our inner life.

In the gospel of Luke Jesus offers a parable about how our inner lives can interfere with and impede the growth of God's Word within us. He describes the Word of God as the seed sown in a field by a farmer, the field being the inner life. Insofar as the heart is opened and fertile, the seed finds a nurturing environment for growth into maturity. Insofar as the inner life is cluttered with the cares, concerns, greed, and preoccupations of the ego-dominated life, the seed will wither and die (Lk 8:5-15). This is a wonderful description of the way in which many of us approach prayer. We simply don't allow the real meaning of the words we pray, or the words we read in scripture, to seep into our heart and take on life and flesh. All too often they are crowded out by concerns and preoccupations, the fear of having to let go of many of our illusions and pretensions. For too many of us it seems an impossible task to change our behavior, alter our perceptions, and fearlessly examine and critique our value system. Believing in the Word of God as the Word of life means that we will have to change and adapt our lives, our behaviors, our value systems, and human relationships to live in accord with a truth that stands in radical opposition to the illusory "truth" of an unenlightened culture. To allow God's Word to take root in our life is hazardous to our way of life. Allowing ourselves to be saved by God's Word means that we can have nothing else.

> The seed is the word of God. Those along the path are the ones who hear, and then the devil comes and takes away the word from their hearts, so that they may not believe and be saved (Lk 8:12).

Others of us entertain fantasies of being prayerful, devout, maybe even holy. We imagine that the spiritual life is one of unending bliss and consolation, sentiment and freedom from temptation. Prayer and spirituality are seen as escapes from the boredom and tedium of day to day life; our quest for God is a quest for consolation. When things get tough, no longer pleasant, we become discouraged and give up our efforts. Jesus understands this very well.

> Those on the rock are the ones who receive the word with joy when they hear it, but they have no root. They believe for awhile, but in the time of testing they fall away (v. 13).

There are those of us who make genuine efforts to pray, but on a deeper level we really don't believe the power of the Word, we lack the trust necessary to really abandon ourselves to the sovereignty of God's will. These are the ones who doubt that God really expects us to abandon all care and concern and trust in the bountiful care of Providence. We cling to our controlling, manipulative ways, our dependence on our isolated and egocentric efforts. Our relationship with God remains conditional and superficial, dependent on things going our way. We don't allow the real meaning to interfere with our established way of life. Our insecurities and need for control remain the dominant motivations for our actions, even our prayer.

> The seed that fell among thorns stands for those who hear but as they go on their way they are choked by life's worries, riches and pleasures, and they do not mature (v. 14).

All around us are people who live a mature life of faith. They are not without pain and suffering, a feeling of abandonment from time to time, worry about expenses and security. They experience desires for comfort and pleasure. But underlying all of this, they have found that there is a deeper wellspring of peace and serenity that surpasses everything that the world has to offer. These are the people in whom the Word of God has managed to penetrate beyond their rational concerns, go beneath their ego-dominated mind to the heart center. They have managed to let God prove the power of the Word as the guiding force in their lives and actions. Thus they live from out of the deep wellspring of a mature faith based on an experiential knowledge of God in their life.

> But the seed on good soil stands for those with a noble and good heart, who hear the word, retain it and by persevering produce a crop (v. 15).

A spirit of prayer, a life of serene trust in God, is not the result of being without distraction, temptation, discouragement, and doubt. Successful pray-ers have had to jettison their need for control, their anxieties and concerns, and their desire for comfort and security. The grace of prayer is the fruit of a series of choices, a ritual of discipline, and above all a willingness to remain patiently trusting even in times of darkness, even when prayer is no "fun" anymore. Prayer is a serious business of growing into an adult, responsible, and fully conscious relationship with God.

All the great contemplative and mystical traditions have grappled with the universal problem of the ego-mind and the ego-dominated will standing guard over our inner life. There are certain basic and fundamental principles to overcome this condition that all agree on. In our tradition the process is summed up in terms such as "Centering Prayer" and the "Prayer of the Heart." These methods of prayer allow us to move beyond and beneath the busyness of the mind and the obstinacy of the will to plumb the depths of the heart center, and to prune out the clutter and tangled under-growth of hearts and minds dominated by demands of our unenlightened cultural ego. There is no way around a serious discipline of praying in season and out, when convenient and not, as much when enjoyable as when boring and disturbing.

We will now explore more closely some of these methods that are found in one way or another in all the contemplative, mystical traditions of the world.

six

Lectio Divina

Our reflections on some of the general principles of contemplative prayer bring us to where we can now begin to consider more particular practices that open us to the experience of contemplation. Hopefully the reader will now understand that the term "contemplative prayer" describes the methods and practices that enable us to move to a deeper inner experience of the presence and action of God in our lives, resulting in lives that bring about a mutual engagement with the divine.

There are many paths to this inner experiential knowledge of God's creative action within us, within creation and history. Traditionally formal contemplative prayer begins when we set ourselves about a regular discipline of encountering the risen Christ in sacred scripture.

It might be helpful to point out here that contemplation, as I would describe it, is not something we do or achieve by our own effort. Rather, contemplation is a result of allowing our awareness to slip beneath the activity of our ego mind to that place within where awe and wonder may break forth and flood our consciousness. It may happen spontaneously as we gaze at a sunset, watch children play, or see the geese fly overhead in formation. I understand and use the term contemplation in a broader sense than we usually understand the term. I understand contemplation as a natural condition of our consciousness when we step aside from the normal controls we usually place over our mind and heart. The rituals, words, and actions of our formal prayers are designed to aid us in slipping beneath our conventional thought patterns to this place of pure simplicity and openness of soul. This is why playfulness and leisure are often associated with prayer and contemplation. If we bring a serious and task oriented attitude to our prayer we are likely to get locked into our ego mind, busy about getting our task done, and deny ourselves the simple freedom of spirit necessary for contemplative prayer. A formal discipline of contemplative prayer, when it achieves maturity, brings about a contemplative consciousness in which we live in a habitual state of awareness, sensitive to the presence and action of God in every aspect of our lives.

When I speak of contemplation in the restricted formal sense in connection with our praying the office or praying sacred scripture, I am referring to that contemplative awareness that may arise as the result of the images and thoughts that may appear as a result of this activity. But here again, we must be aware of the fact that our contemplative prayer lies beneath the ritual, words, and images. We need to be able to intuit its subtle presence and yield to it when we become aware of its presence. This is where a playful, relaxed attitude is helpful. We need to step out of the task mode and take up an attitude of hopeful expectancy for the work of the Spirit. Rituals and words are means of arriving at the contemplative moment; they are never ends in themselves. Therefore even in more formal prayers we need to maintain a certain lightness, a readiness to let go and sink into the contemplative moment. We cannot make it happen by any effort of ours, we simply prepare ourselves to let it happen.

This exercise leading to a contemplative encounter with Christ in sacred scripture is referred to as *lectio divina*, or sacred reading. *Lectio* is the quiet, reflective and slow reading of a chosen passage of sacred scripture. It is characterized by a lively faith in God's presence in sacred scripture and a willing trust that God's Word will enter into and rest in the depths of a soul that is open and docile. Thus, there is an expectant and trusting quality to the reading.

What differentiates this exercise from one of intellectual curiosity and academic study is that this action is essentially an act of religious faith, a movement into a relationship with a living person, the Word that from the beginning was with God, that was God, the Word through which all things were created (Cf. Jn 1:1-5). One doesn't need faith to read and benefit from sacred scripture. Anyone can take up the bible and read it for the beauty and wisdom found there and come away feeling inspired and uplifted, or at least informed and enlightened. *Lectio* requires that we bring a faith in the Word as a direct revelation of God, a revelation that can bring new life and power to one's life. A faith-filled encounter with the Word of God is an encounter of our hearts with the heart of God, and therefore it is a transformative encounter that touches the core of our being.

In *lectio* one doesn't aggressively manipulate the Word or attempt to wrestle the meaning from the Word but simply waits and trusts in patience, possibly re-reading the passage several times. It is helpful to keep in mind that if the Word is active and alive, the Word will penetrate and lay bare the innermost thoughts of the person (Cf. Heb 4:12-13).

We need to understand that we are not talking about God's Word somehow being magically embedded in the written pages of the Bible. Nor do we believe like the fundamentalists that the words of the Bible contain a foolproof formula for success, happiness, and a worry-free life in the world. The words of the Bible, read and prayed with sensitivity, awaken our heart center to the presence of the Word, living, and active, penetrating all creation, but especially penetrating and residing within our own heart center. This prayerful reading allows the true and deeper meaning embedded in the written Word to seep beneath the level of intellect and will, those levels guarded by our alienated ego, into the inner and hidden depths of the soul. Prayerfully reading and pondering the Word awakens us to grasp a reality that is already present within us, the seed awaiting impregnation, conception, and birth into conscious participation in our life. In contemplative prayer we are all feminine awaiting the bridegroom.

Our praying the Word actually restores our mind and will to their proper relationship with our intuitive and affective faculties. Our mind and will are softened and toned by our native intuition and affectivity. And the intuitive and affective faculties are informed and guided by intellect and will. Thus contemplative prayer is an integrating process. The Word that interprets us to ourselves lays bare and judges the innermost secrets of the heart.

Over a period of time, the steady practice of *lectio* allows the Word to become an antidote to the seductive allure of the false values within which we live. As the Word of sacred scripture becomes a formative presence in our consciousness, we are gradually drawn away from our entrapment within our unenlightened cultural value system and align ourselves with God's wisdom, the wisdom that confounds the wisdom of the world. Through the steady practice of *lectio* we put on a new mind and heart conformed to the mind and heart of Jesus. This is far more than abstract ideas rattling around in our head; the living Word of God takes on flesh in our flesh and becomes the life of action in the world. The words of the Lord's Prayer: "may your kingdom come, your will be done on earth as it is in heaven," become a reality in our lives.

The entire process (*lectio, meditatio, oratio, contemplatio*) becomes a heart-transforming and mind-altering exercise resulting in a new way of being present in the world. The mind and heart of Christ continue in our life and action.

Today, these many years after the event, many find it difficult to realize that, beneath the words of the bible, there is a living person who walked the streets of his town, suffered, had relationships, and a family: a person who taught by word and example. Our faith tradition hands on to us the belief that in Jesus, God became one like us to awaken us to the reality of our own potential to grow and develop God-like qualities. Jesus mirrors back to us our own forgotten potential to lead lives of virtue, live in God-like relationships, to bring a God-like compassion and reverence for all creation. Sacred scripture makes present for us—many years removed from the original events of Jesus' life—the words, actions, and images that stir echoes and shadows of our true humanity.

We do not "read" sacred scripture. We "pray" it, that is open our minds and hearts to allow the words and images of Jesus to enter and awaken the eternal reality of God's self deep within each of us, to become the reality we are praying.

Meditatio

The sacred reading exercise is followed by an interlude of meditation *(meditatio)*. This is a time when one allows the mind to prayerfully, imaginatively, and delicately, even playfully, engage in a process of gentle probing for a meaning that resonates deep in the soul. While this is often referred to as a discursive process of the mind, we need to be on guard against a too energetic, aggressive, or intellectual approach to understanding the Word. *Meditatio* is the beginning of a process that is going to result in a personal and unique relationship with God through Christ. Like any true relationship, our heart will be touched at its depths, we will be called forth from our guardedness to risk the possibility of a new sense of self.

The Word is God's revelation and cannot be grasped by intellect alone. While there is some intellectual activity, we need to allow the soul to remain still and quiet so that the deeper meaning of the Word may open the soul and take its rest there.

Meditatio is a threshold process whereby we pass from intellectual activity to intuitive and affective receptivity. The phase of *meditatio* begins with the gentle probing of the mind, but leads to an intuitive understanding, an inner knowing. Therefore we need to be alert and sensitive to the delicate process in which we move from intellectual probing to intuitive knowing. If we gently and patiently allow our minds to quietly probe the Word, we will find that in time the Word will reveal its true and deeper meaning. This happens when the Word read in sacred scripture enters into union with our spirit hidden in the darkness of our inner life. Our inner life is encountered by the inner life and mystery of God who created us by an utterance of the divine Word. God's Word in sacred scripture is a light illuminating our inner darkness, and revealing the living image of God within us, the fundamental truth of our being. This is the beginning of God's Holy Spirit and our spirit joining in a new life-giving union that will bring forth a transformed personality, a new creation in Christ. This is an illustration of the delicate relationship between the Word and Spirit.

The Word of God is eternally alive and self-revealing through the process of material creation and human history, our religious traditions and scriptures. When we allow our souls to rest in silence and solitude, the always active, penetrating and self-revealing word of God is allowed to seep past our usual ego defenses. On this deeper level it searches, probes, and reveals the Word of God nested within the depths of our inner life, lost, forgotten, hidden, and neglected beneath the layers of illusions, distractions and seductions of our daily life.

> The true light that gives light to every [person] was coming into the world.
>
> He was in the world, and though the world was made through him, the world did not recognize him. He came to that which was his own, but his own did not receive him (Jn 1:9-11).

When we open our mind and heart to God, we allow God's Word access to our hidden, inner true self where God's Word is nested as a seed awaiting the revelation of the light. As the Word probes our inner life, God's Word of truth that uttered us into being, the Word that is the fundamental truth of our being, nested within, awakens us to our own inner truth. We awaken to the realization of our innate holy communion with all creation, all beings in God's loving Word of self-revelation that is the ground of all being. Our inner darkness, the darkness of our delusions, social and cultural distortions, is dispelled by the light of God's Word, our vision and understanding pierce the veils of illusion and we "see" from the enlightened center of our being what has always been there.

> Yet to all who received him, to those who believed in his name, he gave the right to become children of God—children born not of natural descent, nor of human decision or a husband's will, but born of God.
>
> The Word became flesh and made his dwelling among us. We have seen his glory, the glory of the One and Only, who came from the Father, full of grace and truth (Jn 1:12-14).

In this contemplative process of *lectio* and *meditatio* we allow room in our inner life for God's living Word to come alive in our flesh. Like Mary, we give birth to God's Word in our life. The Word awakens us to who we truly are and we know ourselves for the first time. Thus, knowing ourselves, we know the true meaning and purpose of our lives, to be temples from which the living God brings love to the world.

We may find that this requires some patience and humility on our part. It is well to remember that in the beginning we are going to be influenced by our ego conditioning and we will want to experience success for our effort. It may take some time before we can quiet our restless spirit to allow God's Word to move past the ego-mind into the heart center.

Another difficult passage we will have to encounter is the dawning awareness that on a deeper level we are really not the person we have come to believe we are and want others to believe we are. Beneath the social pretensions of our learned behavior lies the inner darkness of our hidden self, the self that we have learned to keep beneath conscious behavior. Our path to the life of grace nested within leads through our unconscious and involuntary participation in the broken and frayed fabric of our shared human condition. Our path toward wholeness and truth requires that we recognize, own, and integrate this hidden self into our conscious identity. It can be disorienting and disturbing to honestly recognize and own this hidden shadow self, but there can be no integration, no wholeness, no genuine healing without this painful passage of purification. The end result, however, is a genuinely transformed and integrated personality.

This is the experience from which true affective prayer (*oratio*) emerges. Our prayer becomes a personal, unique, and totally subjective encounter with the Word from which our soul opens up in an utterly personal and unique response to God.

Oratio

Sooner or later the meditation phase will result in some response from our heart. This is the movement of our heart center in response to being stirred by a word, a phrase, or an image evoked by the meditation. This spontaneous movement is our unique response to the Word as it has revealed itself to us in the concrete circumstances of our life; in revealing itself to us, the sacred Word has also revealed something about our selves, our lives, relationships, or actions, positive or negative. It may have stirred some recognition of a subtle sin or failure, a behavior or attitude; we may recognize a neglected or forgotten talent or grace that can enrich our relationships or actions or deepen and enhance our participation in life. Similarly, it may have awakened a response of gratitude, humility, wonder, or awe.

A sense of a need for guidance may arise in the heart leading to a spontaneous prayer of petition. The meditation may have stirred a latent sense of God's goodness in creation, God's love and protection throughout our lives, feelings which give rise to a response of adoration and praise.

We should not be surprised, however, if we experience some strong feelings of remorse, shame, or guilt resulting from a recognition of some habitual sin or failure in our life which we have been minimizing or repressing. Remember the passage from Hebrews: "Nothing in all creation is hidden from God's sight. Everything is uncovered and laid bare before the eyes of him to whom we must give an account" (4:13). The price of genuine prayer is to know ourselves and to be unconditionally known, to be transparent and unprotected by the pretensions and illusions of our egoistic self. A life of grace is buried beneath the layers of denied sin and darkness. Before the life of grace can be realized in our lives, we have to allow the Word of God to shed light on our darkness and sin. While this experience might be at first disorienting and disconcerting, it is not a knowing that leads to depression or self-negation, but to the liberty of one freed from the need to pretend or evade; it is the liberty of one transparent before God who knows the hearts of all and freely bestows divine mercy and redeeming love without condition.

Our experience of liberation may inspire a prayer of surrender into the infinite mercy of God. It may make us think spontaneously of Mary's Annunciation and inspire us to repeat over and over again: "Behold your servant, Let it be done according to your Word," or it may be a prayer from the life of Jesus such as: "Father into your hands I commend my spirit."

The important thing to remember is that, even though we might use traditional words or phrases to give expression to our feelings, our prayer is a personal, subjective, and unique response to the Word as that Word impacts our soul. The heart is stirred, moved by this unique and personal encounter with the Word of God. To put it another way, the Word of God has penetrated our hearts and brought forth an utterly new and unique response. The words or phrases we use are simply feeble attempts to give expression to the inexpressible within our heart. It is an experience of utter intimacy with the source of our being. God's living Word in sacred scripture has found and awakened its counterpart nested within our own soul. The great transcendent mystery of God's Word in sacred scripture and the word and experience of our individual life have intersected. We may come to a point of such trust that we will not even try to find words or feelings to express the experience, but simply allow ourselves to be embraced and taken into the experience.

We need at this moment to be able to surrender to the experience and allow our heart center to take over our prayer until the experience has run its course. This is what is meant by being docile to the Holy Spirit praying within us. Nor should we be afraid to follow the lead of the Holy Spirit in taking our prayer to this deeper and more personal level. It is through this process that God's Word will work its way into the deeper level of our inner life and lay bare and judge the innermost secrets of the heart.

Contemplatio

When our inner life becomes more habitually quiet, more sensitive and responsive to the inner movements of our spirit, more comfortable and serene with the various inner movements of our soul, we will find that *lectio, meditatio,* and *oratio* will lead us into a quiet and peaceful rest in the knowledge of God's Spirit within us. We will discover the truth of the experience of all mystics and contemplatives down through the ages, that is, that our spirit will find its true rest only in union with the Spirit of God, even when that divine Spirit brings with it the purifying pain of the truth that reveals our inner darkness. We will know that eventually the light of God's truth will overcome the darkness of our soul; all we need do is rest in patience and trust. This is the joyful, ecstatic pain of purification and opening to new life in God. This is the state known as contemplation. Contemplation is the quiet rest of a soul that finally realizes that all its effort to love God is futile because even the desire to know and love God is itself a participation in divine life; it is a response to the lost and hidden divine life within. The soul knows intuitively that finally there is nothing left to do but rest all one's efforts in the abyss of divine mercy. It is the natural fruit of all prayer and devotion. It is the state in which our hearts find rest, where inner healing and restoration of spirit takes place. This experience brings peace and serenity to our external actions, our overall demeanor, and our relationships. Real prayer that is allowed to take possession and live deep within our heart center is healing and restorative. Prayer liberates us to live in the fullest possible dimensions of our human life and action.

This deepening relationship with our inner life is an expansion of our mind to encompass an ever enlarging view of reality. We come to an awareness that we can trust our ability to know truth internally; we break through the limits of rational thought to a deeper realm of mystical experience, a more direct way of knowing than is available to us through rational thought alone. Mysticism completes the rational process by integrating the intuitive and affective faculties. Our entire self—body, mind, and soul—functions as a single organ of knowledge. This wholistic intuitive knowledge is the seedbed of Wisdom.

We may find in time that our *lectio* may take us immediately to this contemplative rest, bypassing the *meditatio* and *oratio* stages. If this occurs, we should simply and humbly allow ourselves to be taken into this rest while being careful to avoid doing anything to attempt to prolong it, possess it, and claim it as our own. Our prayer grows and matures into a habitual state of consciousness by an attitude of surrender and acceptance. The grace of prayer is nourished when we learn to let go of our personal desires and expectations, our need or desire for consolation or tangible results.

With perseverance over a period of time, praying when convenient and when it is not convenient, through times of consolation and through times of desolation, we will find that our consciousness remains connected to, and nourished by, these deeper moments of contemplative silence and inner stillness. The intuitive wisdom that is the fruit of contemplative prayer remains just beneath the threshold of our working consciousness, ready to come to our assistance to inform and inspire our actions and decisions. Even in times of trouble and confusion, we will find that there remains readily accessible to us an undercurrent of tranquility and peace that never quite leaves us. With our mind clarified from fixed attitudes and cultural assumptions, we test our intuitive mystical insights over against the perennial wisdom of God's living Word. We become more sensitive to this living Word present in our historical moment.

This residue of contemplative peace and awareness enables us to look on the world and respond through new eyes, eyes opened and clear from the knowledge of the inner experience of God living and acting within us. Nothing substantial has changed, but our heart has found its true resting place where it remains anchored in the peace that cannot be taken away. Pretensions and delusions have been taken away and our sense of self is now grounded in simple, unadorned truth. True and lasting inner peace is grounded in humility. Humility is the simple childlike acceptance of the two poles of light and dark, sin and grace that is our inner life. Humility is a childlike trust that God in the Holy Spirit can weave our inner life into something new and truly beautiful and holy, a transformed personality no longer propped up by pretensions, evasions, and cultural posturings. Our judgments and decisions are made according to the deep truth of divine wisdom now actively a part of our inner life.

We see from this that this form of prayer is an integrating experience. In *lectio* we begin with a very clear act of the will and mind. Our critical faculties are employed. As we move into *meditatio* our intuitive and affective faculties begin to become operative. This leads to *oratio* in which our intellect and will are directed by our affective faculty. Finally in *contemplatio* we move beneath the rational and affective altogether to simply rest as a fish in water or as a bird riding the thermal currents of the air. Repeated practice of this discipline leads to an integration of mind, will, and heart in which our affective and intuitive faculties are joined to our intellectual and volitional faculties. As this practice becomes habitual our life is directed and enriched by this joining of our inner life with our external life. We live life, make decisions, and engage in relationships with a new clarity of mind and heart.

One of the very evident fruits of this integration is the ability to discern more clearly how so much of our life and energy is dissipated on non-essential activities. We become more sensitive to the toxic effects of unhealthy relationships or non-productive situations. Previously these activities and situations might have appeared to be essential or inescapable, but are now seen more clearly as being non-essential and remediable intrusions into our life. As a result of this clarity, we find that we can take control of situations and make changes that leave more time and energy for the important things. In short, we become more discriminating in the use of our resources of time and energy.

While this program of contemplative prayer may seem far removed from the experience of most, it is more accessible than we might at first imagine. A patient, steady, and regular discipline of *lectio divina* with a movement into *meditatio* and *oratio* will soon result in a living encounter with the risen Lord whose life-giving mystery is waiting for us with the Word of God in scripture. We will soon find that creation and the circumstances of our life also reveal to us God's presence in our lives. Life itself becomes *lectio, meditatio, oratio,* and *contemplatio.*

Of course prayer, like everything else in the spiritual life, does not follow a logical or programmatic course. Prayer is the work of the Spirit and the Spirit breathes where it wills. Therefore, one should not be dismayed if their experience of *lectio* does not follow the above described course. Generally one's progress would be expected to move from beginning, *lectio,* to the end, *contemplatio.* But it may not follow in a straight path. In the beginning one may spend considerable time experiencing dryness, restlessness, and boredom before moving to an experience of an affective prayer response leading to an experience of contemplative stillness and rest.

It is helpful to remember that as one takes up the way of contemplation, we are going to have to go through a process of inner detoxification wherein our inner spirit is weaned away from the influence of the cultural ego and inauthentic habits of action and thought accumulated over a lifetime. Our culturally defined ego is accustomed to experiencing a sense of accomplishment, of being dominant and in control even of things spiritual. Restlessness, boredom, frustration and anxiety, a sense of futility and defeat may assail our soul and tempt us to abandon our intentions. Only patient, humble perseverance will enable us to move through to a deeper contemplative prayer.

On the other hand we may find that in the beginning one's relationship with God is characterized by an experience of an outpouring of emotion and sentiments of affection and love. This is often referred to as the "honeymoon" phase of our spiritual journey. In this case we need to be cautious about becoming attached to these gratifying experiences. All relationships are tested and tried over time and through the trial of inner purification. A relationship with God is no exception. As with a spouse or a friend, it is nurtured and burnished through seasons not only of warmth and comfort, but through times of dryness, boredom, loss, and seeming abandonment.

If our commitment to a discipline of contemplative prayer is firm, we will remain patient and persevering even when our prayer leads us into areas of self-knowledge that might cause pain, distress, and an experience of being abandoned by God. The positive results of this kind of discipline will be a transformed personality grounded in the truth of a conscious union with the transcendent Spirit of God now fully active in our life.

seven

Centering Prayer

Centering prayer has recently become popular among the laity. It is based on the work of the anonymous author of the *Cloud of Unknowing*. It is not a devotional prayer as much as it is a discipline aimed at bringing the practitioner to a state of inner quiet in order to be attentive and responsive to the inner movement of the Holy Spirit.

Centering prayer utilizes the breath and a sacred word (such as "Lord Jesus Christ," "Mercy," "God's Spirit," etc.) combined with a recommended body posture to "center" one's awareness. Thoughts, images, fantasies, memories, and feelings are allowed to pass into and through one's awareness without capturing the attention. As the inner material is released from the restraints of the ego-mind, they emerge into awareness and, as one remains focused on the breath and the chosen sacred word, they pass beyond. When we become enticed by a thought, image, or memory, when distraught by anxiety, impatience, or worry, we simply recognize what is happening and gently draw ourselves back to the word and the breath. Gradually, over time and with patience and perseverance, we learn to allow this inner material to move in and out of the field of awareness while we remain focused on the experience of breathing and the sacred word. The aim is to move beyond or beneath mental activity and the use of words or images. What people often consider to be distractions are not considered to be such in centering prayer unless one allows the thoughts and images to capture one's attention. Only when we pay attention to them to do they become distractions. We seek to keep our mind on the breath and a sacred word as the inner material comes to conscious and goes on its way.

As the mind and will relax we may find ourselves in a zone of quiet, inner peace and stillness, where all thinking and willing cease. When this happens we simply surrender to the experience and no longer concentrate on the discipline. When it passes we return to the breath and the word.

Body posture is an important part of the discipline of centering prayer. Effort is made to maintain the body in a state of quiet, remaining still and avoiding all unnecessary movements. We should select a chair that allows us to remain upright with our feet flat on the floor and the upper body erect. The shoulders should be held in a position that allows our breathing passage to remain open and free. The hands should be placed either palms down on the thighs or cupped with the palms upward. Maintaining the body in this state of gentle discipline allows us to move inward and concentrate on the breath and the sacred word. One should not be concerned about physical sensations while in the centering prayer posture. It is to be expected that when we become more silent and still, we will become more sensitive to, and aware of, the physical sensations of the body. When we learn to maintain a regular and steady discipline of the body, we will find that our inner discipline follows. The external noises and movements, and the sensations of our body move to the edge of conscious awareness.

While it is important to maintain a gentle discipline of physical stillness in order to achieve inner stillness, we should allow ourselves to be relatively comfortable. Physical discomfort can be a distraction and impediment to the inner quiet we are seeking. If a person finds that they experience a stiffness or habitual soreness when attempting to maintain a posture, they should attempt to find a more suitable position. While the external physical posture is an important aid to centering prayer, it is not the essential element. If one experiences a chronic pain, stiffness, or soreness, it is important to find a place and posture that will allow that person to move his or her awareness inward.

Centering prayer may be seen as a method of allowing inner space for repressed psychic material to reveal itself, be acknowledged, and then allowed to be integrated into our conscious self-identity. We should not attempt to analyze, understand, or judge the material that rises to the surface. It is sufficient to recognize it, honor it, and allow it to pass on. If we find that we are allowing this material to entice us to dwell on it, we gently bring ourselves back to the breath and the word. It is important to remember that anything that is important for us to recognize in our inner life will eventually make itself known to us again. We shouldn't burden ourselves with trying to remember or understand what is happening during the time of prayer. It is also well to keep in mind that the action of the Holy Spirit is not always sweet consolation and delight. The Spirit of

God led Jesus into the wilderness to confront raw, primal evil, the evil that infects the human heart. Likewise, Jesus, following the lead of the Spirit, went to the Garden of Gethsemane and finally to the cross. In a similar way the Spirit of God must first awaken us to the dark, unintegrated aspects of our personality. This is our wilderness experience, when we encounter face to face, within ourselves, the darkness that holds sway over the human heart. This is the beginning of our path to clarity and internal integration.

Centering prayer is an example of how contemplative stillness acts as a psychotherapeutic process. Just because we have blocked certain memories, incidents, and experiences from conscious memory doesn't mean that these realities of our inner life are inactive. These hidden memories remain active and influential in the way they affect the quality of our perceptions, actions and relationships from the unconscious. We may discover for instance that when we are in the centering prayer practice, feelings of anxiety, worry, and fear may rise to consciousness. This means that these realities are operative within us, beneath the veils of consciousness. They are influencing our actions, attitudes, and behaviors from the deep consciousness. When they come to the surface, we have learned something about ourselves, perhaps to our dismay. We have learned that what we know about ourselves on a conscious level is not always the whole picture. We have learned that the behaviors and values that we take for granted have their origin from within our unconscious, beneath the level of conscious control. This is the point at which our inner life begins to become a fertile field in which the Word of God can take root, purify and transform our personality, and become flesh in our flesh, action in our action.

This is the therapy of prayer; it is the self-revealing quality of prayer and therefore the healing and restorative quality of prayer. This is the path that leads to humility grounded in truth, the humility that enables us to see and recognize in ourselves what we sometimes fear and detest in others. We are moving toward an understanding of Jesus' compassion for sinners, his acceptance and forgiveness of others' weaknesses.

In centering prayer we do not concentrate on the material that surfaces. The very fact that they shake loose and reveal themselves to conscious memory is itself therapeutic and cleansing. Later some of these memories might remain or return. Then we might want to think about them, journal, or bring the matter to our spiritual mentor, but we should never turn centering prayer into a period of introspection or self-analysis. As I said above, what we need to know for our spiritual growth will be given to us at the proper time.

It is helpful for the practitioner to remember that when doing the centering prayer exercise, we should not think in terms of a sequence of breaths and words running from one to the other. We want to move beyond chronological time. Each breath and each word is complete in itself. We want to be alert to the tendency to think in terms of time or the sequence of breaths one following on the other. We want to be totally present to each breath and each word without getting caught in the trap of sequence and time. Centering prayer enables us to "get out of time" and sink into the absolute present, "no time."

This is only one method that many find useful to quiet the heart, to reach a still-point wherein we can attend to the Word of God, where our personal preoccupations and anxieties are laid to rest. This experience is almost impossible to reach without some form of discipline and method that will enable us to overcome the intrusions and obstacles of our cultural conditioning.

Because of this self-revealing quality of centering prayer, I want to draw attention to the necessity of a spiritual mentor. I believe it is imperative for two reasons. First, our perseverance in the discipline is reinforced by having someone to be accountable to. Second, because we may be confronted with some repressed material, it is helpful to have someone who can reassure us and support us as we grow in humility and self-knowledge. We need to be constantly reminded that we are on a path to a more authentic personality. But for that journey to be completed, we will have to go through the experience of having our false self dismantled. I will speak more of spiritual mentors in a later chapter.

We can experience nothing from our inner life that is not already ours, already operative and influential in our unconscious. It is our story, our lived experience. What happens in centering prayer is that this material that has been until now repressed into the unconscious now seeks recognition, acknowledgment, and integration into our conscious self-awareness. This is the transformative process whereby our personality becomes more genuine, more transparent, less guarded. We present ourselves without pretensions of evasions.

Centering prayer groups are an aid to growing in our prayer life. They provide a framework for accountability and a motivation for perseverance. A centering prayer community also provides a means for mentoring and being mentored by more seasoned members. A centering prayer group that meets regularly also has the additional advantage of providing the opportunity for shared *lectio* after the centering prayer practice.

I think it is important to be aware that centering prayer is never intended to be an end in itself, a means to greater calm, a remedy for high blood pressure or insomnia. When we are approaching these contemplative disciplines and rituals from within a faith context, we need to remember that we are engaged in a personal relationship with a God who has been revealed through Jesus Christ. Jesus Christ continues to live and reveal himself in the faith community through the faith and actions of that community. The ultimate fruit might be experienced on a personal level as an experience of contemplative union and an awakening and enlarging of our consciousness with some related gifts such as wisdom, greater insights, calmness, and so forth. However, the test of the validity of our prayer is a greater compassion and generosity, a lesser preoccupation with our personal needs, and a readiness to give ourselves in service to those in need. What might be called the shadow side of centering prayer is the tendency to see it as our personal "self improvement" project; the exercise can become one of self-absorption, concerned with the positive, self-satisfying benefits alone. The only valid fruit of our prayer should be a greater compassion and concern for the well-being of others. Our prayer should ultimately lead us to be less and less the center of our own lives and more open to receiving all creatures into our arena of concern.

While centering prayer is often taught and promoted as a separate method, I have found that it is appropriate and helpful to consider it as a way of leading into the practice of *lectio*. The Word of scripture acts as a counterpoint to the inner psychic material that reveals itself during centering prayer. It also challenges us to move away from considerations and concerns about our personal experience of inner quiet and calm. The only reason we seek this inner space is so that the Word of God may enter and take possession of our souls and lead us to more authentic and clarified actions in the external arena. Our prayer, no matter how consoling, personally healing, and redemptive it might ultimately be, is never ours alone. The only response to our own healing and integration is to show more compassion to those with whom we share our lives.

eight

The Jesus Prayer

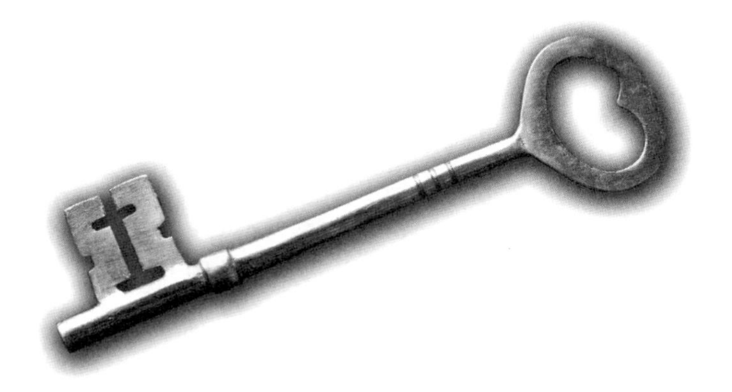

The Jesus prayer is a venerable and ancient practice that comes to us from the Eastern Catholic tradition, especially the Greek and Russian traditions. It has its origin in the New Testament story of blind Bartimaeus: "Jesus, son of David, have pity on me" (Mk 10:46). It emerged into popular use around the fifth or sixth century with the hermit monks of Mt. Athos in Greece. While it was developed in monasteries, it was widely practiced outside the monasteries by lay persons seeking to live a life of prayer. In Eastern Christianity, a mental invocation of the name of Jesus Christ is considered to be most efficacious when repeated continually. It reflects the biblical notion that the name of God is sacred and its invocation implies a direct meeting with the divine. The tradition of the Jesus prayer goes back to the "prayer of the mind." The ancient monks of the desert, particularly Evagrius Ponticus (d. 339), practiced this kind of prayer. It developed in Byzantine Christianity as the "prayer of the heart" and was referred to as *hesychasm*, meaning stillness, a system of continual prayer that sought to achieve divine quietness. This culminated in the ecstatic vision of the divine light and was held to divinize the soul through the divine energy implicit in the name of Jesus. In the thirteenth century, methods of this prayer were developed that incorporated psychosomatic methods, such as joining the words of the prayer to breathing. Through the years the prayer was adapted to the needs of the laity. In modern times the practice of the Jesus prayer was made popular with the publication of the *Philokalia* in 1782 and continuing to the revolution of 1917. It became best known in the West though translations of the anonymous nineteenth century Russian text *The Way of the Pilgrim*.

The Eastern understanding of the notion of deification found its affirmation in the New Testament emphasis on becoming children of God and texts such as the second letter of Peter (2 Pt 1:4), which talks quite unambiguously about sharing in the divine nature.

Like centering prayer it lends itself to people living and working in the world. The Jesus prayer utilizes the breath while reciting the following prayer: "Jesus, Son of God, have mercy on me, a sinner," or some variation of that formula. Some use the shorter form: "Jesus, Mercy." As one breathes in and out the words follow the breath. Repeated over and over again, the soul becomes quiet. It is the experience of many that after a time of practicing this prayer, it becomes habitual and the prayer repeats itself as they drive to work or as they go to sleep or wake up in the morning. Habituation clears the mind from random thoughts and images to allow the prayer to repeat itself at the edges of our consciousness as we engage ourselves in the tasks of our day.

In the Jesus prayer there is an effort to focus on the repetition of the prayer and maintain one's mind and heart filled with the Holy Name. While reciting the Jesus prayer, one attempts to keep one's awareness totally fixed on the breathing and the Jesus prayer. In this case one's awareness is turned completely over to the repetition of the name of Jesus. Functionally, the constant repetition of the Jesus prayer acts as a screen that keeps the hidden memories and unconscious material from becoming the focus of attention during the prayer. Unconscious material may in fact come to the surface during prayer, but one remains intent on repeating the formula and allows the emerging material to simply pass on. Our consciousness is totally absorbed by the repetition of the name of Jesus, while focusing on the breath. In the Jesus prayer repressed material may arise to consciousness at some other time. The end result will be living more consciously from the center and gradually releasing inner matter, resulting in inner purification. Hopefully, over time and with diligent practice, one may find that he or she has developed a habitual awareness of Christ-mindedness that guides one in all one's actions and decisions.

Traditionally the prayer is aided by the use of a rosary of 100 beads of equal size, called a *Kombologion,* used by the Eastern Orthodox of Greece and Turkey. The Russian Orthodox use a *vertitza* which is a knotted rope with 103 beads. This rosary is separated into irregular sections by four large beads causing the lines of the beads to run parallel and form a ladder.

The idea is to keep repeating the prayer over a period of time, keeping the mind fixed on the breathing and the name of Jesus as one passes the knotted rope through the fingers. Through the years the Jesus prayer has gradually become modified and adapted to the use of people living in the world. Unlike centering prayer which requires physical and inner stillness, the Jesus prayer can be employed while walking, running, driving, or any other occupation that does not require mental concentration. It can literally accompany us through our daily activities. Personally I find the Jesus prayer an excellent prayer while driving long stretches of open New Mexico highway, hiking in the mountains, taking long plane trips, or waiting in air terminals. The Jesus prayer has enabled me to patiently endure long transatlantic flights through sleepless nights. The Jesus prayer, I think, is the busy person's contemplative practice. Try it while stuck in traffic. Repeating the name of Jesus throughout the day reminds us that every event of our life is an encounter with the divine invitation to put on the mind and heart of Christ. To return to the scenario of the traffic jam or airport delay, try the Jesus prayer and see how long it takes to set aside feelings of frustration and anger and settle into a tranquil patience. As I said above, the Jesus prayer is perhaps our harried society's road to emotional, mental, and spiritual equanimity.

No matter what method we use however, it must be remembered that the goal and purpose of any prayer is to release the mind and will from the tyranny of the cultural ego and allow the soul to be opened and docile to the work of the Spirit. We must be on guard against the tendency to maintain ownership of our prayer and the process. Whatever we do in prayer, the goal is to move to a moment of surrender to the will of God. Ultimately we want our prayer—the words, thoughts, desires, the entire self—to be taken into the embrace of God's own Holy Spirit who is always praying within us. If we remain too determined to make of our prayer our personal project, we will deny ourselves the very fruit of prayer for which our heart longs and become frustrated and discouraged as well.

In the light of the foregoing considerations, we now understand that a life of prayer is a serious commitment to an inner journey of transformation that ultimately takes us to a life of serenity and inner peace. The journey however, takes us through some inner darkness as we confront the residue and debris of sin and human woundedness that lies beneath the outer layers of our public persona.

Again, in light of the foregoing considerations, it might be well to be reminded how significant and important a serious life of prayer is to our spiritual, psychological, and emotional growth.

nine

The Rosary

The word "rosary" comes from the Latin *rosarium*, "rose garden." It is an exercise in which prayers are recited and counted on a string of beads or a knotted cord. While Western Christians are familiar with the marian rosary, this meditative practice or praying with a set of beads is widespread, occurring in Hinduism, Buddhism, and Islam. The fact that this method of meditation has emerged in many different traditions indicates that there is a universal spiritual principle at work that goes beyond the boundaries of sect and creed. It is universally recognized and accepted as a technique to quiet the mind and open the heart to encounter the divine.

Most historians trace the origins of the rosary in Christianity to third century Eastern Christian monks. It is believed that praying the rosary, perhaps not exactly in the form in which we pray it today, acted as a substitute for the 150 psalms for those who were not able to read. Since that time various forms of the rosary have been developed. In Roman Catholicism the marian rosary became a popular method of public and private prayer. After the Reformation, because of its association with what was perceived to be Roman superstition and ritualism, the Protestant sects abandoned the practice altogether. In more recent times however, with the increased interest in meditation and contemplative prayer forms, I find that the marian rosary is turning up as a valued prayer practice even among many non-Catholics. I have even found several persons who would not consider themselves to be religious in the common understanding of that term, who find the marian rosary with the traditional fifteen decades an effective and cherished method of contemplative prayer.

For those who might not be familiar with the rosary, I will provide a brief description. The beads of the chaplet (rosary), are arranged in five decades (sets of ten). Each decade is separated from the next by a large bead. The chaplet is joined together by a string attached to a crucifix. The string contains three more small beads bracketed by two larger ones.

The rosary requires three turns around the chaplet. Fifteen decades of Hail Marys are recited as the beads are passed through the fingers. Each decade is preceded by the Lord's Prayer and the Glory Be to the Father, recited on the large bead. Each decade corresponds to one of the fifteen mysteries: five sorrowful, five joyous, and five glorious. The mysteries are meditations on the life, death, and resurrection of Jesus.

The origins of the rosary as we know it today are not clear. Tradition associates its popularization with St. Dominic in the thirteenth century. Its popularity both as a catechetical method as well as a popular devotion among the faithful is probably due to the fact that it was an easily accessible means for the unlettered to learn the mysteries of their faith and to pray at the same time.

The Hail Mary itself is a prayer that makes present in our minds the mystery of the Annunciation: "Hail Mary full of grace, the Lord is with thee; blessed art thou among women and blessed is the fruit of thy womb, Jesus." This is followed by a prayer that is a call from the heart center for assistance: "Pray for us sinners, now, and at the hour of our death." An examination of the structure of the prayer will reveal that we have in the Hail Mary the first three steps: *lectio, meditatio*, and *oratio* telescoped into a few words which convey one of the most important and inspiring images of our Christian faith. In contemplation we allow these words and the image they convey to melt their way into the heart where we can simply rest with the mystery and allow it to reveal to us the participation of our life in the paschal mystery of the Lord. If we can say these words with a "soft" heart, that is one permeable and open to allow the words to enter, the Hail Mary can be the threshold to contemplative stillness and rest in the mystery of Mary's modeling for us a fruitful and true human relationship with the divine.

In fact, Mary is the model of the church, and therefore the model for all of us. Her life clearly illustrates authentic prayer, the prayer that we are calling contemplative. Mary was truly attentive, truly submissive to the living Word and was thus possessed by the Word and led into her full and proper participation in God's redemptive act. The Word became flesh in her and through her was given flesh in the world. Nothing captures the true nature of prayer as does this remarkable and dramatic image. Think for a moment of our definition of prayer: ". . . a lifting (or opening), of our mind and heart to God." In Mary we have a perfect living model of what it means to truly pray. We see in Mary the fruits of prayer lived out in a life perfectly abandoned and surrendered to God. Each person, through the opening of prayer, is to become the seedbed in which God's living Word finds flesh. Each of us is to become the fountain from which the Word of God continues to pour forth in love, compassion, and justice into our world.

Meditating on the mysteries of the rosary while repeating the Hail Mary is to travel through the entire life of Jesus to the resurrection, ascension, and pentecost. Again, for those not familiar with the rosary, the prayer begins with the praying of the first round of five decades while meditating on the five joyous mysteries: the annunciation, the visitation, the birth of Jesus, the presentation, and the finding of the child Jesus in the temple. The second round is a meditation on the five sorrowful mysteries: the agony in the garden, the scourging at the pillar, the crowning with thorns, the carrying of the cross and the crucifixion. And finally the glorious mysteries: the resurrection, the ascension, the descent of the Holy Spirit, the assumption of Mary and the coronation of Mary as Queen of Heaven. It is not necessary to pray all three rounds at one time.

Meditating on the fifteen mysteries of the rosary we discover that they mirror for us the mystery of our own life with God through Jesus Christ. The joyful mysteries are full of promise, opening to life and the possible. The sorrowful mysteries lead us to recognize and accept that the way into the fullness of life is most often through suffering, trials, betrayals, and disappointments that are a normal part of our life. Finally, the glorious mysteries awaken an awareness to the reality of the light and life that was nested, awaiting birth within our darkness and unknowing.

The rosary itself is a closed circle of beads, offering an image of the garden. Traditionally, a garden was a walled, protected, and safe place cut off from the dangers and distractions of the outside world. It was a refuge wherein the soul and body could find a safe harbor in which to heal and nourish the soul. The rosary is a prayer sanctuary in which our mind and spirit can find refuge. We enclose ourselves within a protective wall by keeping our mind on the prayer, using the beads as a physical and sensual aid, a guard around the mind and heart.

We prayerfully and attentively move through the garden with the mysteries to protect and safeguard the mind from stray thoughts and random, intrusive images. We open our hearts so that the dreams of our lives are set in relation to the promise and hope of the joyful mysteries. Our pain, suffering, and sense of abandonment, are set against the passion and suffering of Christ in the sorrowful mysteries. Finally we know, through the glorious mysteries, that in Jesus we are led through the darkness of our suffering in life, to the full realization of life in the resurrection.

Another lesson taken from the circular construction of the rosary is the fact that it has no beginning and no end. There is no higher or lower, before or after. Like life itself, the rosary is an unfolding process in which all the parts are simultaneously present and fully operative at every moment. So in the rosary, as we pray the joyful mysteries, the sorrowful and glorious are present, quietly nested awaiting their time to make themselves known.

When we free ourselves from the routine "saying" of the rosary, and simply allow our soul to savor the mystery of God's redemptive love revealed in the mysteries of the rosary and the words of the Hail Mary, we will find that contemplative stillness will eventually envelop us and allow us to surrender to God's entrance into our inner life, to take possession of our soul as God took possession of Mary and filled her to overflowing with divine life. Again, it is a matter of the external words and rituals leading us to experience the awakening of God's own Spirit within us. To get too preoccupied and concerned with the externals, with the proper and complete accomplishment of the ritual, is to thwart the process of allowing the prayer of God's Spirit to pray in union with our prayer. When we feel the soul leaning toward stillness, wanting to be still and rest in the mystery, we should not hesitate to lay aside the ritual and the words, and be still to allow God's Spirit to take over our prayer. When the moment passes, we gently return to the ritual and the words. Like the *meditatio,* the recitation of the rosary is a passage into our interior to meet and be present to the Spirit praying within us.

Because our life is a constant unfolding process, each time we pray the rosary, we are bringing different needs, new experiences, a new level of self-knowledge and understanding, new needs for healing and nourishment. Therefore it is necessary to be attentive to our inner intuitive promptings. At one time the joyful mysteries might attract our spirit and seek to draw us into a healing moment of quiet embrace. We should be free to allow ourselves to rest in this healing moment and allow the mystery to envelop and quietly hold us. At another time one or the other of the sorrowful mysteries might contain the wisdom we need to continue our way through the mystery of our own suffering and perplexity with courage and patience. And so with the glorious mysteries.

The ultimate benefit of the rosary is to provide us with a garden wherein the mystery of God's redeeming act through Jesus and Mary may enclose and nourish the soul as we make our way through the mystery of life.

The rosary is a simple device that teaches us in a very direct way that contemplative prayer and the fruits of an inner life are within easy reach of anyone who will approach prayer with a willing and trusting heart.

To humbly allow oneself to surrender into the routine of repeating the words of the Hail Mary while allowing the images of the mystery to wash through the mind, is to open oneself to union with God's indwelling Spirit. To allow oneself to be taken through the threshold of the ritual to the place where the words and images of the rosary move to the edges of awareness while one is steeped in a personal encounter with God within, is the beginning of a life of deep inner union.

Throughout the history of the church the rosary was a preferred way of contemplative prayer for countless faithful. The entire mystery of the life of Jesus is neatly tucked into fifteen mysteries and the Hail Mary. It is a sophisticated and efficient, if utterly simple, form of contemplative prayer that makes *lectio, meditatio, oratio,* and *contemplatio* available and easily accessible to many who might find formal *lectio divina* beyond their reach. Likewise, it may serve as a prayerful complement to a more rigorous and intellectual study of sacred scripture, offering a restful and prayerful way of allowing the more formal study of scripture to quietly work its way into the heart center.

Unfortunately, through the passage of time the recitation of the rosary became surrounded by a culture of superstition and quasi-magic religiosity for many. At the conclusion of Vatican II there was a shift away from marian devotion as well as other popular devotions, to an emphasis on liturgy and sacred scripture. This was a perfectly legitimate and understandable adjustment to accommodate the higher level of education for many laity. Lay persons were encouraged to study theology and sacred scripture and take a more active role in the ministry of the church. The level of academic and theological sophistication made the Bible and the innumerable commentaries easily available to large numbers of the laity. The recitation of the rosary, along with marian devotion in general, went into decline.

While it is true that in recent times leading up to Vatican II the rosary and much marian devotion fell victim to many unenlightened abuses stemming from a poorly developed religious sense, the rosary for many was undeniably a path to deep interior prayer and contemplative union with healing nourishment for the soul. With the de-emphasis on marian devotion and the recitation of the rosary, many were denied an effective form of prayer that enabled them to touch the deeper wellsprings of the heart center. Rather than look at this decline in negative terms, it is possible to see this period of absence as a positive move toward the recovery of a more traditional and authentic understanding of the rosary. The rosary is an exquisitely simple and accessible instrument of deep contemplative prayer. Now as we begin to see an interest in the rosary resurfacing, we can hope to see that our understanding and respect for this devotion have been cleansed from previous excesses and abuses.

What we are coming to realize is that, in spite of the abuses, the rosary, properly understood, continues to provide a simple and uncomplicated method of prayer that has served the faithful as a path to contemplation for countless generations. This prayer has undoubtedly brought abundant spiritual fruits to the community of the faithful. The dynamic of the method of praying the rosary, if followed, without a preoccupation with "getting it done and getting it done right," incorporate the very same methods used by the mystical contemplative religions of the world for centuries. It should come as no surprise then that a form of the rosary has been a chosen method of contemplative prayer by the great contemplative traditions of the world dating to pre-Christian times. It was picked up and adapted by the early monastics and became an essential tool of their contemplative practice. We dismiss this ancient practice to our peril.

The attentive recitation of the Hail Mary, while meditating on the mystery and passing the beads through the fingers, is a device that enables the mind to remain focused, the heart open and attentive. This is the most effective way to move beyond the intellect and reason and into the heart center to affective prayer (*oratio)* and then into contemplative stillness. Many used the rosary without realizing it to move into deep contemplation, resting in the embrace of the mystery of God within. Many others have walked on the surface of the deep wellsprings of contemplative prayer, but hesitated to "let go" of the need to complete it correctly. As a result the recitation of the rosary remained a spiritual task to get done, a spiritual trophy to claim at the end of the day.

It can be hoped that today, while many Christian souls are looking for a deeper prayer life compatible with their life in the world, this easily accessible and venerable prayer of the faith community may experience a resurgence. Furthermore, with our increased appreciation of the Word of God through the study of sacred scripture, we can again recapture the primary value of faithful and prayerful recitation of the rosary, namely that the rosary is a simple and easily accessible way to delve into the mystery of the Word of God. Furthermore, in our present ecumenical climate we might hope and pray that this excellent and effective contemplative prayer might find its way into those other faith traditions that through their liturgical and sacramental traditions have remained tied to our common contemplative and mystical tradition. Rather than remaining a stumbling block to dialogue, this marian devotion, properly understood and practiced, could become a source of unity.

ten

The Stations of the Cross

The practice of praying the stations of the cross originated in the medieval pilgrimages to Jerusalem. The pilgrims prayerfully walked along Christ's "Way of Sorrow" to Calvary. While the pilgrims were basing their path on the biblical account of the Passion of Jesus, there is clear evidence that the intuitive wisdom of the faithful played an important part in the experience. The creative imagination of the faithful allowed them to embellish the scriptural record, drawing the experience of Christ's passion, through their imagination, into their own affective experience. In this way they took ownership of the prayer by inserting imaginary episodes which made Christ's Passion and death meaningful in their lives.

By the late fifteenth century several incidents that were the result of pious devotion rather than a strictly biblical account became unquestioningly a part of the devotion. The account of the meeting with Veronica and her compassionate gesture of wiping Jesus' face is one notable example. This is also the origin of one of the Western church's most venerable images of the face of Jesus on Veronica's veil. The three falls of Jesus, the meeting of Jesus with his mother, and the removal of Jesus' body from the cross and placing it in the hands of his mother are other examples of how imagination embellished this popular devotion. The image of the dead body of Jesus being placed in the arms of his mother has produced some of the most memorable and cherished art in the Western world. It is interesting, and I think noteworthy, that some of the most endearing images of the stations are not given any mention in the scriptural account.

In order to make the graces of a pilgrimage available to as many of the faithful as possible, and also because travel to the Holy Land was becoming increasingly dangerous, the church eventually authorized the Franciscans, the custodians of the holy places in the Holy Land, to promulgate this devotion in their own churches and chapels. Eventually, the Franciscans were authorized to extend this devotion to other churches outside of their jurisdiction as well. Even until now, although the devotion is not as widespread or as popular as before, the stations of the cross are considered an integral part of church furnishings.

I believe that the stations of the cross are a hidden jewel of our devotional life, a hidden channel that can lead to a deep and fruitful contemplative union with God. They are rich in imagery capable of opening the hidden wellsprings of compassion and humility within all of us. Beneath the images lies the unfathomable mystery of the incarnate love of God. The stark horror of the "*Via Crucis*" of our tradition is the unvarnished truth of God's unconditional love for sinful humankind. This devotion also carries nested within the imagery, the radical nature of the divine claim on the human heart.

The passion, death, and resurrection of Jesus Christ are nothing less than the path to a transformative initiation of the soul who truly wishes to "put on Jesus Christ." "If anyone would be perfect, that one must pick up the cross and follow me." We oftentimes forget that the eucharist, the central image of our faith, is the sacrament that draws us into a most radical participation in the passion, death, and resurrection of Christ. In eucharist we open ourselves to be absorbed totally into the priestly sacrifice that won our redemption.

While for the most part Jesus' closest followers, with the exception of a few women and the beloved disciple, abandoned Jesus during this dark episode, as many of us continue to do today, this journey to crucifixion and resurrection is the journey that ultimately stripped the community of apostles and disciples to the bone, left them utterly forsaken, abandoned, and defeated. They thought they were following Jesus to the establishment of a kingdom grounded in the powers of this world. Instead they found themselves identified with a leader grotesquely writhing in agony on a cross. Their promised one, the one to whom they pledged their allegiance was counted among the criminals and failures of the world.

Even though they fled the scene, they were nonetheless drawn into the confusion, shame, and ignominy of their teacher. They could not escape even behind locked doors. They tried to return to their former life, pick up where they left off, but try as they might they were caught in the whirlpool of the cosmic event that had unfurled itself around them.

And you and I, try as we might, cannot escape the dark reality into which we have been drawn through the suffering, death and resurrection of Jesus. Every time we approach the table of the eucharist we abandon ourselves into this dark drama. Some may be shocked by my use of the term "dark" to describe the drama of the suffering, death and resurrection of Jesus. However, if we pause a moment and attempt to get beyond our cultural bias against the dark side of the passion and death of Jesus, we will be able to confront the stark reality that Jesus surrendered himself into the darkness of human sinfulness and through it entered into the glory of the Father.

When we attempt to deny the dark side of the redemptive mystery, to go around the unpleasant aspect of this mystery of human sinfulness within each of us, we run the danger of a superficial, pietistic spirituality that fails to address itself to our own inner brokenness and sinfulness. As a result we end up with our spiritual life split in two. Our prayer remains on the surface, external and split off from our inner life; our inner life is not brought into our life of faith. The sinfulness that plagues us, our unbridled emotions, our longings, greed, lust, and anger are kept tucked away, unrelated to our life with the Savior who came to take our sinfulness on himself.

We have grown accustomed to a kind of spirituality that might be characterized as an upwardly moving spirituality. That is, a spirituality that urges us upward and away from the less pleasing aspects of our human condition. This upwardly moving spirituality wants to disassociate itself from the sinful, dark side of our experience and relate only to the more pleasing, ego-enhancing side of our public personality, those aspects that win the approval and affirmation of our society. This kind of spirituality is best described as a spirituality of the super-ego. It is a spirituality that seeks to reach beyond our human condition to the realms of idealized virtue, we strive toward a romanticized notion of what we think God wants us to be, a virtue that is untouched and unaffected by our fallen human nature. This spirituality requires that we always keep our best foot forward, our refined, cultural personality to the fore, while our darker side, our sinfulness, our weakness and powerlessness are kept hidden from ourselves, from our neighbors and from God.

This kind of spirituality makes us vulnerable to sudden attacks from the unconscious where run the deep streams of our human sinfulness: our rage, greed, lust, and our unrequited loneliness. We are striving to be someone we are not and can never realistically be. This kind of effort prevents us from an honest relationship with our true, hidden self; we are split from our own center and therefore from our life of conscious union with God. One of the great paradoxes of the spiritual life is that holiness, the light of the divine, does not lie outside and beyond human flesh, but inward, beneath the neglected debris of our alienated ego. Our journey toward holiness and truth is inward and downward through the darkness to the light of the divine within.

The spirituality that comes to us from our most ancient tradition is an inwardly-directed spirituality that opens us to know and accept the deep layers of our human brokenness, our participation in the horrible sinfulness of our human family. This spirituality is that of the Incarnation, the movement of God into broken, sinful, and weak human nature; we enter into a dynamic and life giving relationship with the dark side of our humanity. The ancient desert fathers and mothers knew and taught this kind of spirituality. They went into the desert and wild places where they would be free from the allurements of their culture to face their own inner demons. They became familiar with their inner life, with their participation in the sinfulness that tore humanity at the seams. They recognized that the powers of sin, rage, and human violence against one another and against nature, had their seeds within each one of them. In recognizing and identifying their own sinful nature, they recognized and owned their participation in the sinfulness of the entire human family. In bringing order to their own inner life, they believed that they were bringing order to the entire human family and non-human creation as well. A careful study of the writings of the desert fathers and mothers reveals an extraordinarily profound and insightful psychology relevant to our own time. They knew and understood the operations of our passions. They became healers of the soul and brought peace and tranquility not only to themselves but to countless others as well. We would do well to heed their advice to attend to our inner life to bring order to our external lives.

Through the years a misunderstanding of the term "salvation," or "saving our soul," has taken root in our Christian consciousness. Today it is common for believers to understand this term as referring to our life after death. In fact our earliest tradition, coming from these same saints of the desert, understood no such thing. "Salvation" and "saving our soul" had a direct reference to the quality of our life here and now. Prayer and ascetical disciplines had a direct influence on the way in which one understood and managed one's emotional life, the passions and disordered inclinations here and now. One attempted to order one's life so that one could enjoy peace and serenity here and now. The fruits of an ordered life were enjoyed not only after death, but were available here and now. The spiritual life and the practices that went with it were directed to God through our neighbor. Living well meant enjoying heaven even as we awaited its fullness in the next life.

Just as Jesus entered into our sinful condition, took our sinfulness upon his shoulders and offered himself as a sacrificial lamb to the Father, so the desert fathers and mothers found the courage to embrace their own sinfulness, bring it to the redemptive mystery of God's divine mercy, and share in the ongoing paschal mystery of Christ. Sinful humanity was brought into the redemptive mystery of Christ's sacrifice. Their union with God through Christ was not separate from their union with sinful humanity by recognizing and acknowledging that sin within themselves. This explains why throughout the centuries, men and women of true prayer were always persons of great generosity and compassion. The fruits of prayer were measured only by the compassion expressed toward the needy.

The way into a union with the redemptive mystery of God through Jesus Christ is not away from our sinfulness, but directly into it. We enter into union with sinful humanity by recognizing our sinfulness and in this union, we find our union with Jesus Christ who himself did not disdain our sinful flesh. *God made him who had no sin to be sin for us, so that in him we might become the righteousness of God* (2 Cor 5:21). In the passion and death of Jesus we see in graphic detail how God in Jesus did not hesitate to immerse himself directly into the maelstrom of human wickedness. In the midst of this breaking forth of human sinfulness now specifically directed against him, Jesus gave an example of how the human soul can triumph over sin through love. When we accompany Jesus on his way of sorrow, we immerse ourselves directly into the experience, and if we allow ourselves a moment of truth, we will see how we are one with sinful humanity. But in our sharing in our human weakness, we also share in the promise gained through love.

Meditating on the stations of the cross is a way of imprinting the passion, death, and resurrection of Christ on our minds. Through this imprint our consciousness is cleansed from the egocentric self-absorption of our culture and given a new set of values, a new perspective from which to understand our place and role in our society.

Images reveal truths through a process that transcends the abstractions and theories of theology. Images bypass the cognitive process and address the intuitive and affective faculties directly. There is little chance of the mystery getting entangled in our abstract, rational process and falling captive to the cultural ego. Slowly we find ourselves putting on the mind and heart of Christ. Our mind and heart become the channels though which the will of God is done on earth as it is in heaven, where the Kingdom of God is made manifest in our time.

While the stations of the cross has a recommended method, we need to remember again, that the end and purpose of any devotion or ritual of the church has as its end the opening of the soul to a personal union with God. Consequently, we do well to remain alert to the movement of God's divine Spirit stirring within us as we proceed through the various stations. As in our recitation of the rosary, it is important to remain sensitive and responsive to urgings, to rest with an image as our feelings respond to our meditation. As in *lectio*, we want to remain free to move into our reflective ruminations and allow the image to speak directly to our heart center. As the meaning of the image stirs within our soul, we may become aware of our own special and unique understanding of this particular image and its significance for our life. It is as if the passion happened uniquely for us in our particular circumstances in life. Through any one station, God speaks directly to us in the unique circumstances of our life, our needs, desires, and worries. We should not hesitate to remain with a particular station as long as it speaks to and nourishes our soul. If we don't finish the entire fourteen stations, it doesn't matter, we have encountered Jesus in his passion, our hearts have been touched, our minds opened.

We have been touched and brought into a transformative encounter with the savior of humanity. We have begun our journey to our own participation in the redemption of the world.

To meditate properly on the stations of the cross is to open the heart, mind and will to be penetrated by the mystery lying beneath the image of the particular station. Every event, word, and teaching of Jesus is aimed at awakening us to our own hidden capacity to be loved, healed, and forgiven in order that we might in our time love, heal, and forgive.

We do not pray the stations of the cross in order to appease or placate God, but rather to open our deepest heart center to be probed, awakened, and then surrendered into the ongoing mystery of God's love for all humanity and creation. We seek to surrender our lives into this mystery so that it might penetrate our consciousness, transform our mind, and possess our will. The mystery of God's redemptive and healing love awakens within our own heart center and we then become the sacraments through which divine love, healing, and forgiveness pour into the world.

Meditating on the stations entails a process whereby our selfishness, greed, and petty-mindedness are revealed, challenged, and repudiated. We stand in the presence of the mystery of unqualified and unconditional love and see ourselves as the bearers of the sin for which Jesus Christ died. We come to see and understand ourselves as the bearers of the violence, selfishness, greed, and lust that tears at the fabric of our human family and creation.

If we can see ourselves as the bearers of the toxins of sin that tear at the fabric of the order of creation, we can then see ourselves as the point at which the healing and redemption of the world takes place. We become the sacraments through which the unconditional love of God continues.

As in *lectio,* contemplating the mystery of the passion, death, and resurrection of Jesus means that we do more than gaze at and intellectually ponder the historical event. Through meditation, we open the protective walls of our heart to allow the living event beneath the images to pour into and take possession of our imagination, our emotions, and our mind. We absorb the reality beneath the images into our heart, to confront whatever impedes or inhibits our generous participation in this ongoing divine intervention into human history.

This is a time of personal crisis in which we are given the choice to allow this mystery of divine love to crowd out our self-absorption, to judge and indict our preoccupation with our personal well being, or to allow the reality beneath the image to take up residence in our heart, to recreate us as selfless instruments of the divine will for healing and forgiveness.

It is perhaps timely once again to remind the reader that in order for this self-emptying to occur, it is necessary to lay aside and leave behind all pre-conceived notions about the external ritual and expected results from the proper performance of the devotion. With practice and patient perseverance, we will become skilled at hearing the Spirit inviting us to set aside our efforts, to rest in the consolation of this mystery anointing our soul.

eleven

Eucharist and Contemplative Prayer

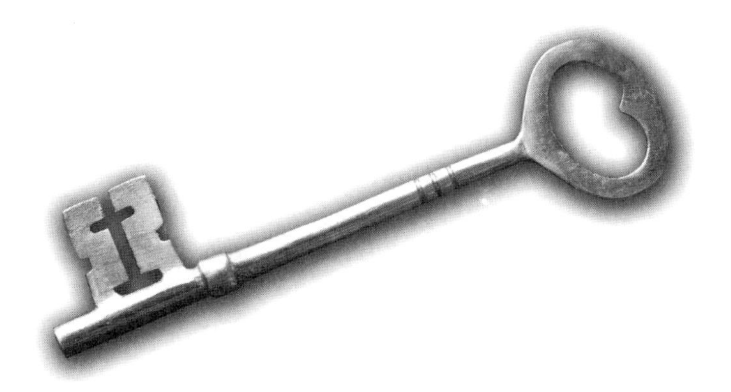

In the Sacrament of the Eucharist we encounter in one dramatic sign the totality of the mystery of the Incarnation, in fact the summation of the entire history of salvation. In the same sign we find the summation of our response to God's loving intervention into human history and the unfolding of the evolution of creation. As a sacramental sign, it transcends the limits of the mind. Its true meaning and fruitful efficacy lies beyond the ability of the human will to accomplish. It is a mystery in the truest sense of the word, a mystery the depths and meaning of which can only be encountered in a living faith. This is not the passive, compliant faith that simply gives up and mindlessly accepts what it cannot understand, but the active, life-giving faith that enables us to reach beyond the frontiers of our human limitations to engage the fullness of life with energy and hope in things known yet unseen. This reaching beyond is not an abdication or diminishment of the realities of our human experience, but the acknowledgment that created reality is on a continuum with the uncreated reality.

The eucharist is at the center, and holds the essence of the contemplative and mystical dimension of our Christian revelation. As such it cannot be grasped in its entirety by the mind alone, but requires the inner knowing that is the fruit of contemplation. The eucharist is the meeting point between God's eternal being and the human quest for meaning and purpose beyond the horizons of our seemingly futile and fleeting existence. As such, this sacrament is the seed within which God's revelation of divine love lies waiting to reveal itself and grow in the life of the believer. The eucharist is the medium of transmission in which divine love is transmitted to become a living reality in our lives and actions.

While our will might be effective in urging us toward this mystery, and the intellect is essential in opening our minds to this mysterious divine action, the ultimate meaning for each of us depends on our accessing the truth of the divine life nested and awaiting birth within each of us. This is ultimately a unique and entirely personal encounter with God. This is an action that brings about and makes real and concrete the personal and unique union of the human heart with God, the source and end for all created reality. Contemplation is the process through which this reality moves from the theoretical and speculative, the formal and ritualistic, to a living, life-giving reality, a new energy, a new impulse to the reality of daily life.

In and through this sacramental action the present day community enters into and becomes a participant in the eternal mystery of divine sacrificial love. Through eucharist, eternal divine love pours into human flesh to become one with the life and action of the believer. The eucharist, properly understood, becomes the passageway by which the believing Christian moves to an entirely new level of consciousness, a new level of being and action. The believing Christian by moving toward the altar of sacrifice to receive the eucharist makes a dramatic and bold statement of surrender into the mystery of God continually entering into human affairs. It is a statement that declares the believer is prepared to take on an entirely new identity, a new way of seeing the world and acting in it. It is the task of the faith community to continue challenging each of us to eliminate the gap between what the eucharist calls us to and our lived reality, internal as well as external. It is the catechetical task of the official teachers to continually remind us of the reality beneath the sacramental actions we perform and the seriousness of harmonizing our life with the reality of the sacrament.

The eucharistic action flows in two directions. In one direction, from above to below, God, through the sacrificial act of Jesus Christ, moves into a relationship of total presence under the form of bread and wine given as food to be taken and shared in a community of friends. In the other direction, from below, the community moves toward the realization of its innate God-like qualities of love and service through the eating and sharing of the body and blood of Christ. Through this movement, each person makes an act of faith (implicit or explicit, depending on the level of awareness each of us brings to the action) in his or her potential for divine union. This is more than a mere theoretical union; it is a substantial union in which God becomes one with our flesh, united in our actions and relationships. In the realization of this union, God becomes flesh again on earth in the body of the faithful. Because of the nature of the sacrament the reality of the divine presence is not affected by the faith or consciousness of the person receiving the sacrament. A nonbeliever could walk into the church and receive the same sacrament as the believer. From the point of view of our emphasis on contemplative awareness, the quality of our conscious participation is important. When the person receiving the sacrament does so with an active, conscious faith, then that person is disposed to give the reality of the sacrament a more dynamic and conscious presence in his or her actions and decisions. The Christian with an awakened consciousness knows that each time the sacrament is received, the life of the believer is being called to judgment. Being conscious also means that one is aware of the discrepancy existing between the reality of the sacrament and the reality of the believer's life. As we are able to consciously enter into this mutual interaction between God and ourselves, we are able to consciously surrender our lives into this mystery. Consequently, we will be more likely to allow the true meaning of eucharist to flow into our lives, purify our motivations, and influence our decisions and actions. In short, we will close the gap between our eucharistic belief and our actions.

This is describing eucharist as a dynamic and creative, reciprocal relationship. It is a relationship between ourselves and the divine, moving us toward a renewed and clarified relationship with the community. Once we open ourselves to this dynamic relationship, boundaries, divisions, and separations of any kind must slowly dissolve and disappear from life.

In the eucharistic meal, the full potential of humanity for union with God in selfless love is revealed and made real in our time. From the other direction, from above, God's generous willingness to become one with human flesh, continuing the action of creation and redemption through human cooperation, is actualized. Our lives, opened and penetrated by the mystery, make us the carriers and transmitters of the mystery of God's saving action in Jesus Christ. In the gathering and celebration of eucharist, the body and blood of Christ are taken into our bodies and transmitted to the world through our life now intimately united with Christ. We proclaim that through our eucharistic actions and relationships, we will grow into the reality we have sacramentally celebrated. Through eucharist we become the body and blood of Christ continuing his life-giving and healing mission. The full mystery of Jesus Christ becomes one with our flesh, alive in our lives and through us continues to touch and redeem humanity. When we allow the full transformative mystery of the eucharist to possess us, our lives become the sacrament of Christ's presence; we become the sacrament we celebrate. The sacred species on the altar becomes the point at which God moves in the direction of persons, and persons move in the direction of their God; it is the point at which we all become one with one another and with God.

> In the most blessed Sacrament of the Eucharist, "the body and blood, together with the soul and divinity, of our Lord Jesus Christ and therefore the whole Christ is truly, really and substantially contained." This presence is called "real"—by which it is not intended to exclude the other types of presence as if they could not be "real" too, but because it is presence in the fullest sense: that is to say, it is a substantial presence by which Christ, God and man, makes himself wholly and entirely present (*Catechism of the Catholic Church* #1374).

The Catholic church has held fast to the belief that in the eucharist bread and wine actually become the body and blood, the true and perfect substance of Jesus, true God and true man. In this belief there is contained the implied notion that humanity is capable of becoming concretely, substantially one with the divine. We become what we eat.

We enter into an essential union with the divine, we become one in our flesh with the divine. But we also, by that very action, become one with one another, whether we realize it, want it, or not. When we share the one bread, take of the one cup, we are one in Christ's body, like it or not. In spite of how we might feel about the person standing next to us, or about the priest presiding, or other racial or socio-economic groups, we in fact become one in the body of Christ. To truly celebrate eucharist, we move into actions and relationships in such a way as to make the substance of the sacrament a tangible, visible reality in our lives. To receive this sacrament consciously erases the divisions and dissolves the enmities not only among individuals, but among nations and ethnic and racial groups. The fact that many continue to receive eucharist week after week, year after year, yet remain so closed within their own bitterness, anger, and resentments is an indication that we have a long way to go in understanding the deeper meaning of this sacrament that is at the center of our Christian belief system. The fact that so many of us can, as a people, make such a concerted effort each Sunday to fill our churches and celebrate eucharist together, yet so readily accept political, social, and religious divisions, so readily acquiesce to our nation's military and economic policies that are quite often oppressive shows that we have not yet allowed the full transformative impact of this sacrament to penetrate our hearts and souls.

The upside of this scenario is that when we finally allow this mystery to take possession of our minds and hearts, we will find that we have once more released onto the world the transformative power of Christ to renew our society and all creation, beginning with conversion and transformation of each of us from the inside out. The spiritual task of the believing Christian is to make conscious the reality that the sacrament makes present. In short, to make the effort to surrender ourselves into the deeper contemplative and mystical dimensions of this mystery that is such a part of our tradition.

The eucharist is the transmitting medium whereby our human nature, with all its sinfulness, its limitations, and its brokenness is united with the divinity. We are released from our human alienation, our fear and suspicion of one another, to become one in the reconciling and healing power of God in Christ. The incarnation, the mystery in which God became one with sinful human flesh in Jesus, continues through this action of the faithful. Before the priest elevates the wine at the offertory of the Mass, he prays as he mixes the water with the wine: *By this commingling of water and wine as one, may our humanity likewise become one with the divinity of Christ, just as he humbled himself to become one with our humanity.* This is possible because of the nature of the sacrament, not our belief or openness to allow the sacrament full sway in our life. The sacrament has the potential to effect these changes in our life. It is up to us to surrender to, and interiorize, the reality we celebrate. When that happens, it is like touching fire to gasoline. Our inner, innate capacity for God-like actions is touched and ignited by the fire of God's love. We become living torches, all of us igniting the world in love.

In the action of the eucharist, the church continues to celebrate our call to be one with the divinity of Christ, not later, not someplace else, but here and now! This being so, the eucharist is a radical statement about the innate and essential nobility and dignity of the human person. Thus, the sacrament of the eucharist is not only an occasion whereby we proclaim and celebrate our belief in God though Jesus Christ, but we celebrate the divine affirmation of our innate capacity to become God-like persons, filled with love and impelled toward loving actions in the world. The sacrament of the eucharist points in the direction of a transformed humanity, motivated by inner wellsprings of divine love released by the transformation of our true inner self. The eucharistic action reveals who we truly are in our inmost hidden self. In the eucharist we celebrate not only our belief in Jesus Christ, but we also celebrate and proclaim together Christ's eternal belief in each one of us. The eucharist reveals and proclaims dramatically our capacity to live in the fullness of God's own divine life.

This mystery of God's love now enfleshed in us is expressed through selfless service to all our brothers and sisters, not in imitation of Christ, but in an essential and transformative union with Christ. The image of God within us is now the ground of our life and action in the world. It is a statement about the call of humanity to achieve our full potential for union with the divine by moving away from egocentric isolation into union with one another and to express this reality through loving service to all. This loving service is a substantial participation in the love of God that is at the heart of the mystery of Christ. Love is the very essence of the Christ event, and through the eucharist we allow the life of God within us, love, to become the wellspring of our life.

Through this sacrament, the love that lies hidden beneath the debris of our human sinfulness, held captive by our alienated ego, is liberated to become the driving force of all our actions and relationships. This is the love that forms the true core of our being, that is the true meaning of being created in the image and likeness of God. To really receive eucharist with a conscious and living faith is to allow the shell of sin that entombs our true intuition to love to be melted away to release the fire of love into our lives and relationships.

Christianity is not a theological or philosophical system conjuring up a better world. Christianity is a gathering of people committed to giving their lives in sacrificial service for a world destined to be the Kingdom of God on earth.

The post-resurrection faithful who received the faith directly from the apostles did not place much emphasis, much less did they venerate, the consecrated elements of bread and wine. The eucharistic action was the celebration of the mystery of Christ becoming present in the gathering of the faithful. It was an anticipation in time of the coming fullness of Christ's body in the community of believers. The sharing of the sacred elements was a sign that they were to go forth and become the mystery of Christ they had just celebrated. It was not that they didn't believe in the true presence in the bread and wine, it was rather that they placed the primary emphasis on the living presence of Christ in the life and action of the community through the sharing of the bread and wine. The eucharistic action shared together was the celebration of the ongoing and unfolding mystery of Christ's life and mission being transmitted to them. For them it was a matter of being eucharistic. The eucharistic elements were the medium by which this true presence was transmitted to the life of the community and through them to the world. For them it was important to be the sacrament they celebrated. If the bread and wine were the medium by which the body and blood of Christ were transmitted to the faithful, the community was in its turn the medium by which this living reality was transmitted to the world at large. The life and action of Jesus, including his sacrifice on the cross, were now being continued in their lives.

When the community receives the body and blood of Christ, Christ is, through the celebration and sharing of the sacrament, equally present in the community as well as in the elements. It is the community that receives the true body and blood of Christ and allows that mystery to be transmitted into the substance of their lives. Augustine's words (from Sermon 272) seem appropriate at this point.

> The bread is Christ's body, the cup is Christ's blood. . . . If you, therefore, are Christ's Body and members, it is your own mystery that is placed on the Lord's table! It is your own mystery that you are receiving! Be a member of Christ's body then, so that your Amen may ring true! Be what you see; receive what you are. . . . All who fail to keep the bond of peace after entering this mystery receive not a sacrament that benefits them, but an indictment that condemns them.

The eucharistic mystery also points to the potential full realization of the God-life within every human being. True devotion to the eucharist requires that we allow our hearts to be opened and moved by the unknown, unacknowledged Christ awaiting birth into life in the most abandoned and despised of our brothers and sisters. You and I are the only means they have of receiving the message of God's unconditional love through Jesus Christ. You and I are that Christ. The restoration of balance in the two-fold mystery of Christ truly present in the eucharistic elements and in the body of the faithful will reinvigorate our eucharistic faith and our participation in the priesthood of Christ.

As we confront the challenges of evangelization in the years ahead, we would do well to reflect again on the enormous and awesome wisdom contained in this central sacrament of our faith. When we reflect on the inner meaning of this mystery we are confronted with the enormous implications for each of us. The central mystery of our faith calls us to believe that each of us is called to accept the stupendous responsibility to become what we eat, to be what the eucharist says we are.

When we consider the inner mystery of the eucharist, several things must be kept in mind. First, the eucharist in the tabernacle or the monstrance is not an objective "it" to be adored, but a life to be lived, an action to be released in the world through our action. Second, when Jesus took bread and wine and told his disciples to "take and eat," "take and drink," this was, is, a clear indication he had every expectation that his followers would receive into themselves the very essence of his life and teaching. They were being given a sign that they were to continue his word alive in their lives, even to the very giving of their life just as he was giving his. It is clear from the Acts of the Apostles that this was their understanding as well.

The eucharistic mystery alive within each of us calls us to move from cheap, easy evangelization of words and proclamations to the heavy, meaty, and costly evangelization of lives lived as priest and victim for the salvation of the world in, with, and through Jesus Christ.

Therefore the altar of sacrifice is the focal point of our eucharistic faith. The elements preserved in the tabernacle or shown in the monstrance for public devotion must always be seen and understood as calling our attention to the sacrifice repeated in the liturgy. It is the action that takes place on the altar that is the focal point of our eucharistic belief and devotion, not the host in the tabernacle or monstrance. Our devotion to the eucharistic species must nurture the intensity of our drive to bring a very tangible compassionate care to every human being and to non-human creation as well.

In our contemplation of the eucharistic elements we are invited to look through them to the action they make present in sacramental form. In our present day contemplative adoration, we see and understand that the eucharistic action of Jesus is to become our action when we eat his body and drink his blood. The eucharist is an ongoing mystery—a life being brought to completion through the ages by the actions of the faithful, the body of Christ. If we do not actively live eucharist, then the mystery dies within us. As our ego triumphs in our lives, as our lives remain trapped within our self-concern, our prejudices, anger, and resentments, then the transforming and redemptive power of the eucharist dies in our closed heart. Our personal time and place is denied the redemptive and transforming action of Christ.

For those of us who might have grown cozy in thinking that our faith and devotion are complete by merely taking and eating and drinking, or simply adoring the eucharistic elements, we would do well to remember the original story. When Jesus celebrated the Passover supper with his disciples, the action that was to inaugurate the New Covenant did not stop with the passing of the bread and wine. Jesus got up from the table and walked into the darkness to complete the covenant on the cross. From the sharing at the table to the cross is one eucharistic action. The passage from the table to the ultimate sacrifice cannot be eliminated from our celebration of the eucharist. Our faith in the eucharistic mystery must include not only the eating of the bread and drinking the wine, but the ultimate shedding of the blood on the cross. When we eat the body and blood of Christ in faith, we enter into this same journey into self-sacrificial love for our world.

In our contemplative adoration of Christ in the tabernacle, we look through the elements to the living reality beyond it to see ourselves being beckoned to walk the same path from the table to the cross of our life of service in the world.

twelve

Sabbath Time

As the pace of society and the demands on our time and energy increase, it becomes clear that religious devotion and practice require significant dedication and commitment beyond the usual routines of conventional Christianity. There is no short or easy path to the heart of the deep meaning of Christianity.

I have spoken at length about contemplative disciplines that awaken us to an abiding awareness of God's presence and action in our lives. Because these practices require that we make choices to stand aside from many commonly accepted cultural conventions and values, the contemplative lifestyle can be considered counter-cultural. It is counter-cultural in the sense that one must make conscious choices to turn aside from many activities that prevent or impede not only a life of prayer and reflection, but a well balanced life that nurtures mental, emotional, and physical well being. The same conditions that impede a life of interior prayer are also known to be serious hazards to our mental, emotional, and physical health. Therefore, whatever practice nourishes an inner life of prayer is also going to have a beneficial influence in other areas of our lives. Contemplative practice also makes good sense for mental, emotional, spiritual, and physical health.

In a culture that highly values the productive use of time and energy to enhance and embellish our material self-interest while proportionately de-valuing "down" time, silence, study, prayer, and reflection will certainly be seen as odd. It is difficult to step aside from the cultural flow and stake out a place for the development of our inner life. However, in failing to see to this personal imperative, many of us are paying a steep price in emotional, spiritual, and physical dis-ease, as well as suffering the consequences of shallow and unfruitful relationships, even our relationship with God. This is true not only for people living the life of lay persons, but for vowed religious and priests as well. Many of those called to ministry as vowed religious and ordained clergy have been completely absorbed into the collective mind soup; a non-think acceptance of the manic pace of an unenlightened society. When the shepherds, teachers, and leaders of the faith community are nourished on the cheap fast foods of conventional religion, then the faithful are going to be proportionately malnourished. Oftentimes we have to experience a crisis of meaning and purpose before we will find the courage and energy to stand aside and take stock of our situation and make the necessary changes. These changes often require sacrifice.

It will not take long to realize that contemplative practices reap their own measurable benefits that far out-weigh any material loss or sacrifice of social standing. The benefits in peace of mind, reduction of stress and tension with an experience of general all around well being are hard to measure in conventional terms. But more significantly, a life grounded in a living awareness of our true value, a value and meaning that transcends the limited horizons of our chronological life, is the ultimate pay-off of contemplation.

One practice that ranks high in its ability to bestow spiritual, physical, and possibly material rewards is the custom of carving out Sabbath time in one's life. This is not easy in a culture that values ceaseless action and measurable productivity. The Hebrew covenant, the Christian covenant, and the subsequent history of our Judeo-Christian tradition give abundant evidence of the consistent communal value of Sabbath time, time taken from the usual rhythm of daily labor and preoccupations to dwell on and ponder the things of God. By this time we know that to dwell on the things of God is to ponder the deep meaning and purpose of our own truth. Our physical, emotional, spiritual, and psychological well being is God's work. Whatever service we do for the world is built on the foundation of our own self care. Our first ministry of care for our world is to see to the harmony and integrity of our own life. The greatest teaching a person can give to the world is the teaching of a well-ordered life, grounded in a well-articulated value system.

We need to be careful to guard against our modern Western biases when considering the meaning and purpose of this steadfast and universal practice of Sabbath. Examining the passages in sacred scripture that deal with the Sabbath practice we find that it bears none of the anti-world, anti-matter prejudices that arose in the practice in our own recent pre-Vatican II history.

A careful reading makes it clear that Sabbath time imperatives in the Hebrew scriptures are guided by a clear understanding of the sacred quality of human relatedness, even extending to a reverence for the natural rhythms of creation manifest in the earth. In Leviticus, there is a call to allow the land a Sabbath rest.

> The land itself must observe a sabbath to the LORD. For six years sow your fields. . . . But in the seventh year the land is to have a sabbath of rest, a sabbath to the LORD. Do not sow your fields or prune your vineyards. Do not reap what grows of itself or harvest the grapes of your untended vines. . . . Whatever the land yields during the sabbath year will be food for you—for yourself, your manservant and maidservant, and the hired worker and temporary resident who live among you, as well as the livestock and the wild animals in your land. Whatever the land produces may be eaten (Lev 25:2-7).

Everyone, even the wild animals have a claim on the bounty of the earth.

Sabbath time was never completely unrelated to one's life in relationship to the earth and the community. In the Hebrew scriptures the earth, work animals, servants, slaves, and aliens all benefited from this sacred interlude in the rhythm of ordinary life. All benefited from times of rest and restoration. This illustrates the basic principle of the Hebrew covenant, namely, that the observance of God's law extends to all areas of one's life. God's law as revealed in our sacred scriptures is a law that connects and harmonizes all aspects of our lives on earth and in our relationships with all others reaching through non-human creation to our relationship with God. Observing God's law connects us to the law of our human nature, the inner law that brings peace and harmony to our lives and relationships.

In Deuteronomy 5:12-15, the Sabbath obligation is placed in the form of a commandment. No work is to be done by son or daughter, manservant or maidservant, ox nor donkey or any animal. The alien within the gates and all servants are to have a day of rest. Finally, this imperative is put in the context of the deliverance from slavery. "Remember that you were slaves in Egypt and that the Lord your God brought you out with a mighty hand and an outstretched arm. Therefore the LORD your God has commanded you to observe the Sabbath day" (v. 15). While the laws and their specific objectives were written and observed within a specific cultural and historical setting, we should not use this as a way of excusing ourselves from the application of their underlying principles to our specific time and place. The underlying principle of maintaining a harmonious and mutually life-giving interaction between ourselves and our world remains valid for us today. The laws governing the rhythms of creation and our individual lives remain operative. To ignore these laws puts us and our world in danger. What is required of us is a creative and courageously innovative interpretation of the principles and their application to our particular circumstance.

The principle function of the observance of God's law, including the law of Sabbath, is that it dethrones our alienated and self-centered ego from its tyrannical rule over all our actions, perceptions, and relationships. Sabbath time dismantles the structures that recognize the labor of men and women as no more than instruments of economic and political interests. Sabbath time reestablishes a proper relationship between human labor, the natural rhythms of creation, and the sovereignty of the Creator and the creative process. It places us within a context of interrelatedness and interdependence with other persons and creation. It reminds us that we are custodians, stewards of the autonomous nurturing forces of creation. Our ego-dominated wills and minds do not dictate the work of our hands. The fruits of our labor are to be distributed equitably. Our labor in life is to be directed toward the maintenance of the nurturing function of the earth; our compassion for all creation is the means by which the resources of creation are to be distributed equitably to all. It is the quality of our compassion that determines the quality of the life of the planet.

This is what makes it so difficult to truly undertake a spiritual discipline and engage in a serious relationship with God. We have to give up our personal primacy and accept our role as cooperator within a context of interdependence, not only with other persons, but in the work of creation as well. We have to stand against the cultural and social forces that idolize unenlightened interests and the competitive forces of materialism, militarism, consumerism, and other self-indulgent pursuits that deplete the soul and exhaust the natural life-giving and life-sustaining forces at work in nature. Our spiritual, psychological, and physical sickness today is symptomized by the rapidly increasing exhaustion of our material environment and the accelerating depletion of earth's resources.

Sabbath rest is one of the foundational laws governing our relationship with God, and there is a strong communitarian element to it which extends to all members of the community, even to aliens, slaves, the animals and the fields (Ex 20:8-11). Taking time out gave an opportunity to put one's relationship to God right, to place one's role and function within its proper context of a cooperative partnership and a mutual effort in the work of the earth. Sabbath time reminded the faithful that God is sovereign in the work of creation, that aliens, one's neighbors, work animals, slaves, servants and aliens all had inalienable rights under God. No person's needs took precedence over the needs of others. To disregard their innate nobility and their rights under God is to disrupt their natural relatedness to the earth and to God. No single animal or person is without their own innate dignity and rights independent of their relationship to us. The Sabbath imperative of allowing work animals, slaves and fields to rest, reminds us that we are care-takers, custodians and stewards; the human person does not have absolute rights over others or over creation. Nor do we have absolute and unquestioned rights over the fruits of our individual labor. We are called to live and labor in such a way as to share the benefits of our labor with others, including non-human creation. The creative, life-giving, and nurturing work of the earth benefits as well from our rest and celebrates its own autonomy and innate dignity.

We can imagine how Sabbath time—giving time back to God—in our life within this traditional context has the capacity to radically re-order our priorities, and allow us the opportunity to place our relationship with God within its proper context. This time of reflective refocusing the way in which we relate to our family, community, coworkers, others with whom we share the universe, material creation, and animals, would bring about a significant shift in the way we see our place in the world. We are reminded that the God of our revelation is a God who is sovereign in all aspects of life, not to be relegated to the margins of life and work and communal relationships.

When we examine the quality of our present day relationships with the earth, with our neighbors, with the marginalized and disenfranchised of our society, we might begin to see how Sabbath time might influence many of our attitudes and values for the better. We might begin to awaken to the fact that many of our social, political, and personal ills are really of our own making, and therefore within our capacity to remedy by changing our attitudes, perceptions, and values.

When we reflect on the level of stress and the incidence of stress-related illnesses in our society, it is hard to deny the benefits of a time of programmed and ritualized withdrawal and rest, a time to reflect on and observe the flow of life and creation continuing without us. We get a glimpse of the autonomous, life-giving flow of creation and an understanding of the balanced and harmonious way in which we are called to insert our presence. Sabbath can be seen as a rehearsal for death; life and creation will go on without us. We can relax and free ourselves, others, and creation from our compulsive need to control that which ultimately cannot be controlled.

Sabbath time does not have to be a solemn, joyless time. In the beginning there might be some anxieties and discomfort related to shifting our gears and letting go of our engagements; the intensity of our resistance may serve as an indication of our attachment and dependence on busyness and engagement.

Sabbath time may be a time of more pleasurable and celebratory activities with family or spouse. It can be a time in which our relationships are stripped of all artificiality, when we turn off such things as television and radio, telephone, and computers that get between us and others, us and creation, us and our inner life. Without these contrivances we can settle into the simple pleasure of being with family and spouse, friend or lover. It can be a time of the pure simple joy of being with those we love and cherish. It can be a time when, with family, spouse, or friend, we may take the time to travel to a place where we can enjoy the contemplation of God's wondrous presence in creation.

We should not hesitate to be creative in our use of Sabbath time. Jesus himself took liberties with the Sabbath by healing (Lk 13:10) and by allowing the disciples to gather grains of wheat for their nourishment (Mt 12:1). When he was criticized by the Pharisees, he gave them a long lecture on the real meaning of Sabbath as opposed to an excessively legalistic observance, an observance that puts all its emphasis on the external observance while ignoring the harmful effects to the soul. We should approach our Sabbath observance as a time of healing and restoration for our soul, our mind, and body.

Jesus healed and did other good works on the Sabbath. We might balance out the interior aspect of Sabbath with a visit to the elderly, homeless shelter, or some other corporal work of mercy. Following the example of Jesus this may serve to remind us of our interconnectedness to one another and our call to receive others into our lives and our relationships with God.

This is Sabbath observation on a level which can significantly enrich and deepen our relationship with one another and with creation. On another level, there might be time alone for prayer, reading, study, or a personal creative project with the possibility of later sharing and mutual enrichment. While American Christians take some satisfaction in being churchgoers, there is also a down side to this predilection for Sunday church. We can fall into the trap of believing that we have fulfilled our Sabbath obligation by this sometimes distracted and routine observance.

Over the years as our society has grown more urbanized and the demands on our time and energy have increased significantly, we have shifted almost the entire weight of our religious life to the church, and this principally for forty five minutes or an hour on Sunday morning. At the same time the family unit and the sacred precincts of the home have been significantly diluted by the TV, the telephone, and the World Wide Web. The spiritual authority of the parents has been handed over almost entirely to the school and the local church and all of this concentrated within the school day, a church service, or religious instruction class. These splinters of time are expected to counteract the saturation of TV, the mall, movies, arcades, billboards, and a multitude of other influences bombarding our consciousness from the time we get up in the morning until we retire.

I am suggesting that an effort to reclaim Sabbath as holy time will help restore the balance and restore the home. We should not restrict our Sabbath observance to the hour or so we spend in church on Sunday. It could very well be that with the busyness, the impersonal crowds that characterize many church communities, going to church may in fact be an impediment to the real spirit of the Sabbath. On the other hand, to reclaim our spiritual authority, the spiritual authority of the parents in the home with home-centered Sabbath time, we might be able to offset the otherwise impersonal busyness and remoteness of many parish observances. Parents are the primary spiritual caregivers in our society, and the home should be the principle place of spiritual formation, prayer, and worship. Churches and church activity should be an aid to establishing the sanctity of the home and the holy task of parenting.

The deepening enrichment of such a practice, the development of spiritual sensitivity resulting from the practice of Sabbath in our homes and families will bring about an enriched participation of our public worship on Sunday when we gather with the community. We will have tapped into a deeper level of our own spiritual life as well as an experience of a new kind of relationship with the poor, forgotten, and marginalized in our midst.

Our spiritual, emotional, and physical well being requires that we take steps to safeguard personal and family integrity by providing ourselves with quality Sabbath time which will allow us to experience and reflect on our needs for relatedness with the deeper currents of our spiritual life within, as well as the deeper spiritual currents of creation and society around us. Eventually we will find that life is all one and that as our interior life is brought into play in our relationships with one another, creation, and society, our understanding and experience of God radically changes. We experience life, religion, and God as an interconnected web in which all of the various strands come together and influence one another.

We are living in a time when we can no longer sit back and assume that because we are following the common mind set and conventional practices of our cultural environment, we will be doing the right thing for ourselves and our world. In previous times it appeared that we could assume that our political and religious leaders represented the collective wisdom of our civic and religious community. We are awash in unmistakable evidence that the "mass-think" of our society today is leading us deeper and deeper into trouble for ourselves, our society, and the earth. Unfortunately, many of our religious institutions and their leadership are infected by this toxic thinking. Mental, spiritual, and emotional burn-out, along with a spiritual malaise, permeate all levels of our society. Rage, frustration, depression, and anxiety are rampant through all age levels, socio-economic classes and professions.

Our time calls for courageous and creative initiatives to reclaim personal authority for the quality of our lives and begin to restore balance and sanity to our lives. As I mentioned before, our service to the world begins by restoring integrity and inner peace to our own lives.

thirteen

Chambers of Silence

The great mystical and contemplative traditions through the ages have valued silence and personal solitude as essential to attaining wisdom. Before the rise of organized religions, the shamans and medicine people found their calling in the silent solitude of the wilderness of mountains, forests, and deserts. In their own way they too encountered Wisdom and contributed to the universal human quest for truth and a deeper understanding of what it means to be human. They were the threshold through which the will of God was communicated to the people. Their lives and teachings reminded the people that there was an unseen world with its own wisdom and truth as real as the one in which they lived.

I understand wisdom to be that divine eternal truth that emanates from the deep inner being of God and which resides in a hidden way in all creation. This divine wisdom in one way or another has been communicated to humans throughout the ages. Christians believe that this eternal Wisdom was fully present in Jesus Christ and was poured out upon the earth at pentecost and now dwells within each of us through the Holy Spirit (1 Cor 2:10-16).

Deserts, mountains and wilderness serve as powerful images of places where the divine is encountered. In the silence and solitude of desert, mountain, and forest, without the support of cultural props, the transcendent core of the person awakens and slowly emerges through the sheaths of our cultural conditioning. In these places of silence, without the intrusion of political, religious, and cultural influences, the consciousness opens inward and downward to the pure truth of the human person. The props that hold in place the personality forged by our cultural environment slowly melt away to be replaced by a sense of self, grounded in a reality that extends beyond the surface and transient illusions of our tribe, family, or national identity. The external props and internal structures of our false personality are useless in the silence of our chosen solitude; the frantic and tyrannical cultural ego is disengaged. Our consciousness is released from the harness of cultural and acquired religious imperatives and allowed to open itself to the deep interior spaces where our unique truth is waiting to be acknowledged and brought to consciousness and action in our life.

Since the early emergence of the religious consciousness men and women have sought the wilderness, mountains, and deserts to pursue a wisdom that lies beyond the horizons of human intelligence. In the vulnerability of deep inner silence, one encounters the true self that transcends the frightened and fragile self that is the product and prisoner of our learned imposed cultural value system. From within this womb of the true self, men and women have emerged with a renewed sense of what it means to be a person in their time and place.

Striking examples of this are Moses, the prophets, Mohammed, John the Baptist, and Jesus. All of these men spent significant periods of time in the desert where the soul and God can embrace in freedom. And of course the entire nation of Israel was led into the desert where for forty years they were formed into a new people. In the time of the Christian covenant we have examples of how men and women would flee to the desert to seek wisdom in solitude only to be followed by countless seekers intuitively drawn by the magnetism of their purified personality.

Out of this heritage, we have a tradition of going into the desert to encounter the reality of the god image within and allowing that inner truth to become the ground of our self-understanding. I remind the reader to understand this God image, the divine image in which each of us were created, not as a static, philosophical concept, a poetic image or theological construct, but rather as a dynamic and creative, ever-unfolding component of our human nature. It is a creative participation in the life of God that allows God to be revealed in a unique and irrepeatable way in each of us. Our lives, actions, and relationships become grounded in this transcendent reality. Our pretensions and posturings, our masks and personas fall away and we stand in the world transparent and simple. Our embodied life is an empty vessel ready to receive the living waters that bring life and light not only to us but to all of those with whom we share our life.

Silence and solitude are something other than static theological concepts, mere rituals, or ascetical practices that have no bearing or effect on our inner life. Silence and solitude are much more than pious practices of the devout anxious to please and placate their God. They are transforming disciplines that integrate our fragmented self to bring about the emergence of a whole person from the debris of our futile attempts to create a self in the image and likeness of our cultural gods. These practices allow us to approach the living God within and nourish our life from the very source of all being and becoming. Patient perseverance in humble silence and courageous regular interludes of solitude allow us to move inward to become consciously one with the source of all being to discover the truth of our *self* for the first time.

They have a specific impact on the quality of our emotional, psychological, spiritual, and even physical lives. Like fasting for the body, silence and solitude are the fasting of the cultural ego. Our life is cleansed and clarified of all lies and pretensions, our mind and heart are freed from delusions and self-deceptions. From deep within, where truth lies, we see the world and our place in it with clarity.

In silence and solitude, the ego is disengaged from its frantic effort to maintain its authority over every thought and action. Previously repressed psychic material, which the ego-self considers unacceptable, is released into consciousness, altering our self understanding and increasing the depth of self-knowledge. Because silence and solitude reveal to us areas of the inner life's experience previously kept from awareness, we have the opportunity to integrate this matter into our self-understanding. We know our self more authentically. This refreshed and purified self-understanding becomes the foundation of humility and a capacity to understand and accept others more compassionately. Because silence and solitude are healing and restorative it is possible for us to say that silence and solitude are psychoanalytic and psychotherapeutic. Personal authenticity and the integration of our inner lives with our outer self-presentations are the end products of a life in which silence and solitude are an integral part.

To say that silence and solitude are a process is to say that their effects are cumulative. The longer and more intense the experience of silence and solitude, the deeper and more profound is the effect of their psychoanalytic and psychotherapeutic action.

The process of this fundamental spiritual discipline is multi-layered. That is to say, as the length of time increases one experiences deeper and more intense effects on the inner life. Likewise, as one's practice becomes more a part of daily life over a period of time, one will experience significant changes in the way in which one lives in and interacts with the world. This is because over time, as one becomes more accustomed to the experience of silence and solitude, one's assumptions about self-identity and one's place in life change. Some relationships are seen as inauthentic, maybe harmful to oneself and others; aspects of one's life might now be seen as grounded in the false self; values shift and one sees the efforts to contribute to the world, or take from it, need to be realigned. As a new sense of self emerges into consciousness, perceptions change regarding reality and the meaning of life.

For the sake of convenience I describe the deepening process of silence and solitude in terms of "chambers of silence." Each chamber has its own unique characteristic and there are specific obstacles or "walls" that must be confronted before entering a specific chamber. It needs to be understood that this is an artificial construct for the purpose of facilitating discussion and understanding of the levels of silence.

The first chamber of silence is one that is basic and essential for mental, psychological, emotional, and spiritual health. This first and most basic chamber of silence consists of those moments when we withdraw to engage in some soul nurturing activity such as reading, writing, listening to music, or engaging in a hobby. Much of our prayer and spiritual practice occurs in this chamber. The essential ingredient here is personal time and space in which one is alone, not in the company of others no matter how intimate one's relationship to those others might be. It is to be noted however, that in this first chamber, all of our actions, even our prayer and other spiritual practices, remain under the control of the ego. The ego-dominated mind remains the operative influence that determines just what one will do and for how long. A characteristic of this chamber is that we judge the quality of the experience in this chamber by the values of the cultural ego. We usually describe the experience in this chamber as being "productive," "satisfying," or in other ways "acceptable." We expect something in return for the time and effort we put into it. We judge it positively according to the degree of satisfaction we derive from the experience.

This is the chamber of minimal essential health of soul, spirit, mind, and body. One who cannot withdraw from human companionship to dwell with one's inner self, no matter how brief and fleeting it might be, will be denied the richness of his or her own poetic, artistic creativity nested in the inner recesses of the hidden self. There is mounting evidence that our physical well being is related to our spiritual health. Thus, we might assume that by taking personal time, Sabbath times, we not only nurture a healthy emotional, social, and spiritual life, but physical health as well.

The "obstacle" or "wall" to this chamber is the need to be around others, the need to be busy, engaged in the socially approved enterprises of the ego. One feels too important to let go of engagements, relationships, or other ego centered enterprises. The "party animal" is a good example of the person who forever camps outside the first wall of silence, afraid to leave behind superficial relationships and engagements for fear they might disappear or slip from his or her grasp. But the "party animal" is an extreme example. Our society is filled with persons who, the minute they find an unfilled space in time, run for the TV, the radio, the phone, or some other distraction that anesthetizes the shock of being alone and disengaged from the accustomed social props. In the religious realm it is all too common for religious workers to be so caught up in the multitude of demands that they find they have all but abandoned any semblance of personal time, not only for prayer and rest, but time for necessary study. The cell phone and pager have become standard for the pastor or parish worker who has achieved the ultimate accomplishment of making themselves indispensable. Religious activism can be deadly because we may fall into the trap of believing that the action of being religious is therefore necessarily God's work, when in fact we are indulging our self-will.

The result is that silence and personal solitude become sources of anxiety, restlessness, guilt, and a sense of loss and deprivation. These feelings are symptoms of ego-deprivation. The activities that keep the ego engaged and in charge of one's life are suspended and its tyrannical authority over our life is denied and threatened. The personal ego rebels at this deprivation.

The one who embarks on a spiritual quest and encounters this wall to the first chamber might feel that silence and solitude are impossible tasks and revert to a more superficial and less taxing spiritual way. One might rationalize that this kind of spiritual practice is self-indulgent, that one has an obligation to be out and about doing God's work. One may feel selfish by denying friends and coworkers his or her presence for the after work social hour.

The way through this wall is to recognize and acknowledge the tension, to be with it, not judging or struggling, but allowing it to speak to the deeper self, revealing the alienation that exists between the outer ego-self and the true Self within. The first inner chamber is achieved not by fighting the tension, judging it or being shamed by it, but by honoring it as a statement of the true condition of the relationship between the inner and outer self. One courageously and patiently endures it knowing its source and its toxic effect on the soul. This tension and anxiety is a messenger of our spirit telling us of matters that need attention from within. The wise person sees these symptoms not as adversaries, but as messengers of light inviting us to make corrections on our journey to spiritual maturity.

As we discover that these feelings and tensions do not have ultimate authority over our actions and decisions, we find ourselves relaxing into calmness, content to be with ourselves. The concern for the opinion of others and concern about the well being of our engagements begin to diminish as we discover that we can get along without controlling the world, and the world can get along quite well without us. We discover a life beyond the nervous imperatives of the cultural ego. As a result our soul begins to grow and express itself in more creative ways, our mind is enriched, our heart is opened to the poetic mystery of the world in which we live. Our work and relationships become more authentic. Gradually we hunger for more silence, more nourishment for our soul and mind. We have moved through the wall to the first inner chamber.

As we grow accustomed and peaceful in the first chamber we discover that another wall of resistance presents itself. The ego begins to nag at our conscience. We begin to worry about "time wasted," not being productive. We tire of reading and have exhausted our ability to keep ourselves, our mind, and heart engaged.

Many people stop at this chamber not realizing that there is more waiting beyond this wall. For this reason many allow themselves to live their spiritual or intellectual life in the shallows of the first chamber dominated by their ego hungering to regain control.

The way through this next wall is to recognize it, acknowledge the tensions of guilt and the need for productivity. We identify where it is coming from and what purpose it serves: sustaining our cultural ego. This awareness enables us to make a choice to turn from the seductions of the ego and remain still, to allow the experience to pass around and beyond us. We withdraw authority from our ego and re-establish our inner authority over our decisions and actions. Our decisions are made from a space of freedom rather than the demands of the cultural ego and the feelings of guilt, shame, and boredom it sends out, seeking to seduce us to surrender to its rule once again.

In the second chamber we put aside all activity and allow ourselves to simply be in stillness, silence, and total presence to ourselves without prop or support. At this point even reading the Bible can be set aside in order to await the emergence of the Word of wisdom from within. Now the ego is totally disengaged. We enter the wilderness place without defense, totally vulnerable and transparent to our inner true Self. Now we move from mere external silence and solitude to the inner silence and solitude where we hear the quiet pulse of our hidden, inner space.

As we allow ourselves to be drawn into the inner silence of the second chamber we discover a deeper freedom from our attachment to ego activities. The peace comes not from their cessation and total quieting, but rather from our freedom from them. We allow them to be and to go on their way.

As we remain in this inner stillness, with the clatter of our ego mind now receding to the margins of our awareness, we discover that recent memories begin to emerge, memories from our recent past that we may have tucked away beneath the layers of our everyday consciousness. The memories might be of painful experiences in our relationships, perhaps a sense of shame or failure over some personal weakness or shortcoming.

Our tendency is now to run from this pain, this unrequited tender spot in our memory. Many people will say to themselves that they don't need or want to dredge up painful memories about which they can do nothing. What we need to understand is that the emergence of this painful memory or memories is an indication that they have not been integrated. We have marshaled our ego defense mechanism to anesthetize them and tuck them out of awareness. They have been allowed to remain in our deep memory festering and awaiting their opportunity to make themselves known and integrated into our conscious self-awareness. They want to become an acknowledged part of our story.

This is a healing moment, a moment of reconciliation with our human frailty and the inevitability of the suffering connected to human relationships. We are delivered from the delusion of believing that we can make life and our relationships perfect and pain free. These memories enable us to become more reality based and less defensive.

This is the wall that stands between the second and third chamber of silence. Again, we do not achieve the inner stillness and deeper silence of the third chamber by obliterating these realities, but accepting them as a part of our lives. We allow them to speak to us and impart their wisdom and humility to dissolve their sharp edged pain. The pain is ego-centered pain. When we disengage the ego and place these painful memories in the context of self-acceptance and forgiveness, they cease to be adversarial and become messengers of wisdom and humility beckoning us to a more integrated and authentic presence in the world.

As we make peace with this buried matter, we discover a new level of calm; we find we can rest in the knowledge that we don't have to fear these assaults, but can recognize them as sources of new wisdom and a truer self-knowledge. We have now entered the third chamber of silence. We have traveled our own inner desert. We have encountered our inner demons and faced them down. We have become more accustomed to our inner landscape. It ceases to be a threatening wilderness and becomes instead a fertile garden watered by the well-springs of our inner life. We are closer to the source of divine light and wisdom. Our inner demons have taken on the face of angels of light promising a life of serenity grounded in eternal truths. The seductive enticements of the fleeting illusory fantasies proffered by our culture are revealed for what they are.

The third inner chamber now reveals another wall standing in the way of still deeper and quieter inner tranquility. We now begin to get closer to more remote memories of early childhood. We begin to experience the torment and distress of more primitive energies which we have learned to repress since infancy and early childhood. We might experience forgotten loneliness, fears, rage, sexual urgings that we learned to fear from parental and religious training. Early experiences of abandonment or real or imagined abuse might begin to surface. Because of cultural conditioning we might have learned to fear and despise these aspects of our personality or our history because of the fear of punishment, abandonment, and rejection by parents and even by God.

These very human and necessary energies split from our conscious awareness. We disowned them as a part of our personality. Painful experiences may have been buried in our deep memory because our fear and shame left us with no way to integrate them into our sense of self.

This is perhaps the most difficult and dramatic obstacle to that inner place of unshakeable peace and security that nothing in the world can take from us. We have entered the fourth chamber. At this point we become anchored in the deep still ocean of God's loving and faithful presence within us. It is the place where our lives and the eternal divine become one. As we make peace with this deep aspect of our inner lives we realize that we share in the brokenness and sinfulness of humanity. We stand as one with sinful, broken humanity, one in our need for the healing and reconciliation that only God can give.

The peace of the fourth chamber is not the peace of believing that we are without sin or blemish, but the peace that comes from the courage and humility of knowing that we are one with humanity moving toward wholeness even as we experience our imperfection. This is the peace that the world can neither give nor take away. Our peace is now anchored in the bedrock of perfect, unqualified self acceptance, even those parts of our selves that had previously been the source of anxiety, shame, and fear. We no longer stand in judgment of ourselves or of others but know the presence of divine love which forms the essence of our being and the source of our unity with the human family and creation.

Now we are open and ready to be penetrated and judged by God's living Word that is spoken of in the epistle to the Hebrews.

> For the word of God is living and active. Sharper than any double-edged sword, it penetrates even to dividing soul and spirit, joints and marrow; it judges the thoughts and attitudes of the heart. Nothing in all creation is hidden from God's sight. Everything is uncovered and laid bare before the eyes of him to whom we must give account (Heb 4:12-13).

Our silence and solitude have brought us to a holy communion with our human family and creation that transcends the fleeting unity of physical communion. Our sense of oneness with others and with creation is nourished by our unity with the divine within each of us. When our inner lives are cleared and opened to the full presence of the divine within us, we are one with the source of divine light and wisdom. This is the inner freedom and light known by all the mystics and contemplatives of all traditions and which is available to us as well.

When we fast from food our body complains and lets us know it resents the deprivation. The result of this fasting however is a body cleansed and clarified, detoxified from the residual poisons which have collected over time.

Similarly, our ego needs fasting. Our ego needs to be delivered from its attachment to external, toxic nourishment. The constant activity of its engagement, its incessant need for affirmation and sustenance from the delusions of culture, serves to screen and filter the emergence of our inner life in union with the divine. As a result every inner experience that does not flatter and support the ego is repressed and denied existence in our conscious self-understanding.

Ego fasting allows time for our inner life to become active and grow into maturity. This activity releases energy previously expended in ego-defensiveness and allows new waves of creative energy to flow into our conscious life. Our external, conscious life now becomes nourished by creative imagination, spontaneity and humility. We open our conscious life to the inner wellsprings of wisdom, the wisdom that is untarnished by the defensiveness, posturings, and pretensions of our ego self. Our ego is now at the service of the true self, the divine self within. We have opened up our inner life to reveal the deep inner place of which Paul spoke in his first letter to the Corinthians. The Spirit that knows the inner mystery of God, that gives us the mind and heart of God, is now accessible to our spirit. The mind and heart are now open to be infused with the light of Christ. The ego now becomes the organ that gives expression to our true Self. We are new persons in Christ and our actions become the channel through which Christ continues his redemptive mission to all creation.

We realize that the true authority of our life comes from within, where our spirit encounters God's Spirit. All external experiences, no longer subject to the judgments of the ego mind, now become means whereby our inner life is enriched, our inner wisdom deepened. As our inner life is deepened and enriched, our outer life of work and relationships becomes burnished by an inner peace. The calm tranquility of knowing who we are at the depths of our being permeates every aspect of our life in the work a day world. We become zones of peace for our time and place. The separations between inner and outer, time and eternity, sin and grace, God and Self are dissolved and all become one in and with the eternal divine.

While I referred in the beginning of this section to the great mystics and teachers of our tradition, it needs to be emphasized that silence and solitude are not reserved to these exceptional persons only. They were exceptional in the degree to which they gave themselves to this practice, and therefore their lives and influence were to that extent exceptional. Silence and solitude in themselves are not exceptional. As I observed earlier, there is today a growing recognition of the necessity for everyone to have periods of time for soul nurturing; time to tap into the deeper strata of the inner life to avail oneself of one's intuitive and affective capacities, to reflect on what is happening in one's life, to remain sensitive to the subtle indications of things calling for attention. In being attentive to these inner voices we might avoid many situations that would otherwise grow into spiritual and emotional emergencies. Regular periods of private time, brief though they may be, can work wonders on the quality of our daily life. The devotional disciplines such as centering prayer, the Jesus prayer, the rosary, and the Stations of the Cross are traditional exercises aimed at assisting us toward an inner and outer silence and solitude.

True, in the beginning we may have to exert some creative effort in finding ways to work this into our routine. As difficult and as challenging as it may be, many are finding it quite possible and the rewards for doing so far outweigh the cost. A careful and honest scrutiny of our days will reveal for most of us ample evidence of time that we usually squander on non-essentials disguised as social or personal imperatives.

Another thing to understand is that we have to be realistic, honestly so, about what life's situation will allow. Young parents or those embarking on a new career are not going to have the same opportunity as persons who are more established in life. The thing to keep in mind is the necessity of establishing a belief and value system early so that we can grow into our spiritual lives as our situations change. For this we need a fundamental mind change; we need to dispel the idea that life's value is judged by the quantity of effort put into arbitrary social imperatives, and replace it with a notion that life's quality emerges from one's firm grounding in the absolute truth of one's core self. We need to move from hearing all the external voices in our society as absolute truth and recognize the infallible truth of our inner wisdom reminding us of who we are at the center of our being.

With this mind shift, personal time, silence, and solitude become the inner imperatives that call us and lead us to the truth of God's life within.

fourteen

Spiritual Mentors

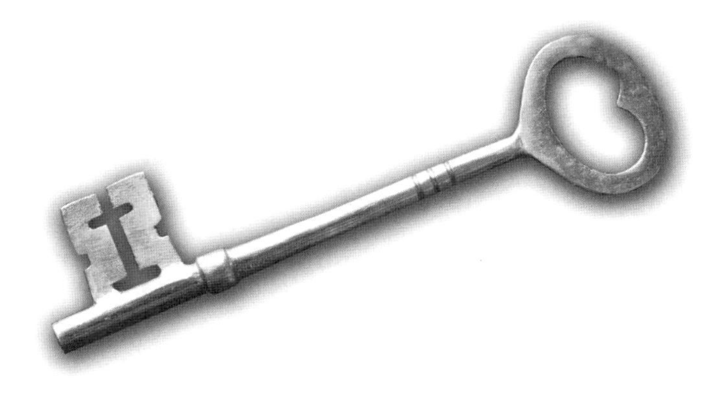

Taking into account all that has been said about contemplative prayer and the necessary changes in lifestyle that accompany it, it is clear that one should not attempt this journey alone. There is much room for discouragement, confusion, and error. It is well to have a guide or mentor to accompany us through the difficult and sometimes discouraging early stages. When we commit ourselves to a regular discipline of contemplative prayer, we are embarking on a spiritual passage that will take us into unfamiliar, and at times disconcerting, inner territory. We are going to discover things about ourselves that have remained hidden behind layers of denial and avoidance.

This is not a reason to avoid contemplative prayer, but is rather a motivation to persevere because the end result will be a personality grounded in truth, cleansed and freed from the pretensions and postures of our cultural ego. It is this process of deepening inner self-knowledge that clarifies, reconciles, and heals the fabric of our true Self. We begin to live more authentically, grounded and nourished by the hidden inner well-springs of our whole Self. We embrace and honor the entire spectrum of our personal, but denied and unrecognized potentials, negative as well as positive. We are led to recognize and take ownership of our hidden and unrecognized sinfulness; our repentance and self-giving to God are grounded and motivated by a newer and deeper self-knowledge. Humility moves beyond the theoretical and academic; from mere pious sentiment, we move to an experiential knowledge of our participation in the broken, sinful condition of humanity. At the same time we come to understand that we participate in the life of the divine that we share with all creation. We awaken to the reality of our heretofore unacknowledged participation in the holiness of our humanity and creation. We begin to experience our potential to be the channels of grace and wisdom, to be lights for those around us.

For all of these reasons, it is imperative to find a guide who has walked the path of his or her own inner journey to the truth of their life. Having walked the path and met their own inner demons, as well as the presence of grace, they have the experience and courage of true humility to walk our inner journey with us, to call us forth when we would hesitate, support when we waver, to guide us in our discernment. Without this guidance from an experienced and humble guide, our path is strewn with obstacles and dangers. With an experienced guide we are able to recognize and manage the many possible dangers that seek to snare our still active cultural ego.

Praying on a regular basis with a contemplative prayer group, using scripture as the basis of shared prayer, serves as an alternative or complement to a mentor. Each person's response to the selected passage of scripture is that person's gift to the community and is received and accepted as such, non-judgmentally, non-critically. The advantage of praying regularly with a group is similar to having a mentor. There is a regular and dependable source of personal accountability, support, and encouragement. Beyond this there is the advantage of having available the collective intuitive wisdom and experience of the group for discernment when one might feel the need for making decisions, or discerning the subtle movement of the Spirit in one's life.

We live in a culture that looks with suspicion on the inner life of the spirit. We have relegated the serious spiritual seeker to the margins of our cultural consciousness. When we are praying regularly in a group or have access to a spiritual mentor, we have available to us a source of affirmation and encouragement to stretch ourselves to explore new and larger possibilities for ourselves in our spiritual journey. We know that we have the support and understanding of other like-minded persons who know the struggle involved in standing against the tide of cultural values. We also have available the opportunity to be monitored and cautioned about our limitations.

Today much conventional religion seems to favor settling for Sunday morning spirituality, tidiness of creeds and conventional, socially approved virtue; the kind of behavior that does not interfere with life in the fast lane or our chosen career track. Oftentimes one hears someone expressing a heartfelt desire for a deeper prayer life, a more adventurous and stimulating spiritual life, but only occasionally do we witness someone actually move from talk to action. This is because a sincere opening of our lives to prayer, and surrendering our will to the divine will, carries with it the necessity of allowing our lives to be judged by a new standard. The standard of the gospel is in radical contrast to the values and beliefs that we may have unreflectively accepted as unquestioned truth. A spiritual mentor or a prayer group affords the opportunity for ongoing discernment by like-minded and equally committed persons who know and understand us well.

The initial stage of the contemplative journey opens our eyes to see the world and our life in it from an entirely new perspective. To follow through on our commitment will require us to take steps that are in radical opposition to many of the values and beliefs of our culture, beliefs and values that we have unreflectively accepted and put our trust in since childhood.

If we have grown up in a society that values and rewards an incessant, unreflective, and uncritical engagement in the manic pursuit of material comfort, security, and power, it takes strong motivation to find time for personal silence, solitude, and reflection. Especially when on the other side of this threshold, there may lie the possibility that we will have to give up and turn from this behavior. Silence, solitude, and reflection begin eroding much of the ground upon which we have established our lives and relationships. Silence, solitude, and a more reflective, meditative stance toward life are the first essential steps toward awakening our soul to an active and creative participation in our life.

In a similar fashion, when we have learned since childhood that it is acceptable only to "put our best foot forward," it takes courage to honestly face into and acknowledge the less pleasant and socially unacceptable aspects of our personality. Often we have managed, through the cultural conditioning of rewards and punishments, to repress many, if not all these personality characteristics, which are now hidden not only from others, but often from ourselves as well.

To begin to open ourselves to our hidden life means we must be willing to acknowledge this less pleasant side of ourselves. There can be no true humility, no genuine freedom until we honestly and courageously allow our hidden, repressed personalities to come into consciousness. The way into the heart center, where God's Spirit dwells, where our human life and God's divine life merge and become one, leads through the inner chambers where our denied sinfulness and human brokenness await the truth of God's redeeming Word. To experience this in the presence of one who knows and accepts us unconditionally is not only an aid, but a necessity.

This is the inner journey of awakening through which we become aware of our personal participation in the brokenness and sinfulness of our human family. Gone are the illusions of superiority, self-righteousness, and complacency that have shored up and supported our carefully fabricated cultural personality. True humility, grounded in this painful revelation, begins to unfold into our conscious self-understanding. Slowly we build a sense of self established on the total reality of who we are at the core. We present ourselves to the world around us as we know ourselves to be, without evasions or pretensions. The person whose inner life is truly present to consciousness is appropriately secure in their relationships with others. The person whose inner life is actively present and operative in their conscious life is free of the need for the affirmation of others, the acclaim of recognition, or the other trappings of social recognition.

However, this can be a disquieting and lonely journey in the beginning. Being free from the illusions of the cultural persona means that we are going to have to let go of many of the assumptions and comforting beliefs that have supported and motivated many of our actions and relationships. It is normal to go through a period of disorientation, uncertainty, and doubt about many of our previously held beliefs and assumptions. We are likely to feel that the ground on which we have securely stood is no longer stable or trustworthy. For those of us who have been taught from childhood that the only reliable authority is outside us in socially approved authority figures, it is quite intimidating to recognize that there is an inner authority, an inner truth and wisdom capable of guiding one's life and actions. This does not mean to say that we totally repudiate and reject all external authority; it does mean that we relativize it, judge it critically according the norms of common sense and intuitive wisdom, given the circumstances.

The costly side of this inner authority means that I can no longer mindlessly flow along according to the latest craze, the latest word from on high, but must actively take responsibility for the quality of my life and actions. Spiritual maturity does not allow for victim roles; nor does it allow for uncritical childish dependence.

If we stop to think about it, it can be no other way. The life and teaching of Jesus call us to live according to a radically different set of values than those our society presents to us. When we allow the light of the gospel to shine on the reality of our lives, we should expect to see glaring discrepancies between what we claim to believe and the way we live and relate to the world. We will find that many of the values that motivate our lives and support our relationships and endeavors are in direct opposition to what the gospel teaches.

This experience of "awakening" can bring about a sense of confusion about who we are, what our life is all about, and the meaning of life in general. This is a significant and critical moment of conversion in which we stand on the uncertain middle ground between what life is at this moment, and what we feel called to be by a higher standard. What we have believed and trusted in the past is now seen as empty, but we don't know quite what lies ahead. If I am not the person I thought myself to be, then who am I? Is there another truer self waiting to come forth? What if I turn from the self I think I am, and find nothing to take its place?

This is why we need a mature and seasoned spiritual mentor to guide us through the chambers of our inner life. One who has walked the path before us is able to gently and surely guide us through the times of uncertainty, doubt, and discouragement. True spiritual mentors are known and recognized not because of the words spoken, degrees and certificates possessed, but by the recognizable quality of their lives, serene, at peace in the knowledge that all humans are called to stand on the secure ground of their inner lives where God is encountered as the source and end of all.

In the past, local parishes were gatherings of neighbors and friends who had shared the same community for years, where children grew up together and attended the same schools, and the community was guided through the cycles and seasons of the liturgical year. The major epochs of life—birth, marriage, sickness, and death—were surrounded by ritual and a firm belief that somehow life had a purpose. Our parish family provided us with the structures and dependable and predictable rhythms which offered us a safe container within which we could stretch or rest our spiritual muscles as we felt necessary. Life, prayer, and communal worship blended together as one. Today however, families are mobile and locations change frequently. Parishes, in many instances, have become once-a-week impersonal gatherings. Funerals and weddings are no longer community events in which we all celebrate the mystery of our own life.

All of this highlights the essential need for a solid grounding in a personal inner spiritual identity and the need for finding or establishing intimate communities of prayerful and wise support as we face the challenges of today's world.

While this fragmentation of our world, our communities, and sometimes our families is painful to experience, it can also serve to highlight our need for knowing who we are and the ground we stand on; for seeking out and establishing intimate communities of friends who share the same values and experience the same need for spiritual support and nourishment.

While many experience keenly the alienation of our society and our institutions, including schools and churches, many are experiencing the life-giving support of regular, at least weekly, contemplative prayer meetings and the intimate support of a spiritual guide. These encounters go beyond theoretical discussions and seek to move deeper into the inner realm of contemplative prayer and a more profound understanding of our sacred scripture and our personal and unique response. What many find, to their surprise, is that periods of silent prayer and silent reflection on the Word of God have the unexpected effect of deepening relationships and establishing friendships on a level of intimacy that far surpasses the richness of their experience elsewhere, sometimes even in their families.

It is ironic and paradoxical that what so many in our society seek vainly in the fleeting liaisons that pass for friendships in the workplace and social gathering places is available in gatherings that value stillness and silence. Perhaps we can hope that from these increasing contemplative groups there will flow out to our society, our families and churches, the calm serenity and inner peace that can serve as a balm for our wounded human family.

Similarly, one who has a committed relationship to a spiritual mentor will soon find that the affirmation and support that comes from this bond of mutual trust, bears fruit in a sense of well being with a deep sense of self-assurance. Self-knowledge and the unquestioning acceptance that comes from one who knows us intimately leads to a personality that is free from the need for approval or the affirmation of our social environment.

fifteen

A Final Word

I have attempted to present contemplative prayer in a way that confronts the difficulties, while at the same time stressing contemplation's necessity and relevance for all of us today, religious, clergy, and laity. I am convinced that the contemplative and mystical aspect of our Christian spiritual heritage needs to be reestablished as the norm in our everyday practice. Christianity is a path to a fully-awake consciousness, boldly engaged in building a just and peaceful society. I have attempted to show that genuine Christian prayer and worship leads to contemplation and a mystical perception of the world. Rather than a flight from the tasks of the world Christian mysticism leads to a radical stance of responsibility for the condition of the world.

No longer can we afford to sit back and believe that God is going to do it for us. Nor can we afford to indulge ourselves in the naive belief that our designated teachers and leaders have the necessary stuff to do it for us. That is not their mandate. Jesus came to empower individuals by awakening each of us to our God-like capacity to create the world according to the divine law written in our hearts and in the heart of creation. One person, Jesus, showed us what it means to be a human being, one with God and with the truth of creation. Jesus now stands on the leading edge, the outward horizon of what all of us are called to become. He is the human person reflecting fully the perfect image of God. In his historical flesh and in his concrete actions with his contemporaries, Jesus opened for us and revealed the hidden mystery of God-like qualities nested deep within the folds of our inner life. To follow Jesus is to follow him into these deep hidden inner recesses of our inner life to discover Christ's life in us and bring it to birth in our flesh.

Indeed, it is a mighty and daunting challenge. But to look at the condition of our world, the decaying of our physical environment, the unraveling of our social fabric, the coming apart of families, the impotence of many of our religious institutions, the violence of our schools, and the trite shallowness of our political institutions, without the hope that our faith brings is to not see the whole picture. We turn to the ancient truths and values, the beliefs and practices that have transformed the world and changed the course of history before and we know we can do it again.

I am not suggesting a reactionary and regressive move to the past, but a clear and creative move into the future, grounded in the conviction that we are each in our own way the creators and healers of our world. We need to honestly admit that the world as it stands is of our own doing, or perhaps the world is symptomatic of our passivity and neglect. The condition of our world is the result of our belief that it was up to someone else to make things right, our belief that God only wanted our docile and passive acquiescence to the status quo.

For those who might feel that a program of contemplative prayer is too demanding on time and energy, I would only ask that they take some time to reflect on the time and energy demanded by many of the intrusive engagements and demands placed on their life by circumstances. We accept many of these intrusive social imperatives as non-negotiables over which we have little or no control. We unconsciously and mindlessly adapt to the demands of our culture and our social environments and find ourselves surrounded by a web of "obligations" and expectations which we had no part in negotiating and which we have never really thought through or owned in a profound and meaningful way.

This, I believe, is symptomatic of our industrialized, electronic society's belief in the authority of external structures. We have slowly moved into a belief system that tells us that all truth, all authority, and all wisdom come from outside of us. The unintended consequence of this stance is that all responsibility lies outside of us also. Other persons in positions of authority and power, traditional structures and institutions, traditions and customs handed on to from previous generations, all have the power and the right to dictate our actions, beliefs, and choices. Thus, when things go wrong or don't work out as we would like, we indignantly blame the politicians and religious leaders or anyone else we think should have been doing something. Little credence is given to our inner authority, our intuition, or innate wisdom. Thus, whatever everybody else does must be right no matter how it might go against my own sense of what is right for me or my family. What the media promotes is seen as a personal imperative. Polls are given the authority to dictate the words and actions of politicians, to influence how we think and make choices about what to wear and what car to purchase. Ultimately, we allow these external voices to influence the quality of family life, the values that dictate our most intimate relationships.

I suggest that for many of us, a brief reflection on our own experience of these external demands will indicate a subtle but real dissatisfaction with many of them. Possibly we may discover that we have been hankering for a way to modify their demands on us and our family. Perhaps we have found ourselves thinking and wishing that we could enjoy more "quality" time, more family and personal time, but felt that we were obligated to keep up the social, political, and perhaps even the "religious" pretensions of our society.

With the escalating demands on our time, the rampant incidence of stress and anxiety with all of the related symptoms in our time, it might be opportune for us to question our allegiance to a set of social values that demand everything and return nothing in the way of peace, satisfaction, and a sense of well being. It might be these very symptoms that are signaling us that it is time to reclaim something of our lives, our time and energy, to re-establish ourselves as the custodians and stewards of our lives. Now may be an opportune time for us to re-establish our family, our friendships, and the quality of our inner lives as our primary task, therein finding the life-giving relationship with a living God.

When we arrive at the end of our lives, we will be totally alone in the solitude of our uniqueness before our conscience and our God. There will be absolutely nothing standing between us and our full awareness of the quality of our lives and the consequences of our decisions. There will be no defensive veil protecting us from the consequences of our decisions and choices, perhaps decisions and choices made under the pressure of unenlightened social imperatives. It may come as a shock to many that in fact we are responsible for these choices even though we made them without sufficient reflection. Reflection or not, we carry the consequences with us and these choices subsequently influence other choices. Sin and its punishment are not so much the act of a whimsical God, but rather the result of our having been given the freedom to choose, and our having ceded this freedom to the tyranny of our social, political, and yes, even our religious institutions. We will not be able to say that we sacrificed our soul, the quality of our relationships, and the quality of our time because we were being obedient to the unenlightened demands of a society and culture that sapped and drained our energy, our time, and our spirit, all the while devaluing the things that nurture our soul. The culture we so ardently obeyed, so thoughtlessly served, will already be cultivating others to consume in our place.

A contemplative lifestyle, a life of conscious awareness of the presence and action of God in every aspect of our life, the innate sacred quality of every least aspect of our life, is our natural religious heritage. Our sacred scriptures, both the Hebrew and Christian revelation, are tireless in their efforts to awaken us to the fundamental reality in which we are immersed; that is, the God of our revelation is a God in history, a God whose very Spirit is within us and within creation drawing all things into unity with the divine. We have been living in a time in which the sleeping state has been seen as normal, in which darkness has disguised itself as light, where true wisdom is seen as folly. Beneath this web of deception there lies the truth. Contemplative prayer, a contemplative lifestyle, living in the counter-culture of the gospel, is the norm for those of us who recognize the God of Abraham and Moses and the definitive revelation of that God through Jesus Christ. To take the time and make the effort to turn aside from the rush of events around us and remind ourselves of the ultimate truths of life and the purpose for which we are here is to do no more than to heed the cry of our own inner self for recognition, the heart's longing for its own source and end.

Contemplative prayer is the only path to the living waters for which our heart longs. These living waters are resting quietly within us, awaiting the opening and cleansing that contemplative prayer and mindful living will bring. Many of us today are thirsting for the living waters even as we stand at the well. We stand right at the well containing the living waters that can refresh our soul, but look above and beyond it to see only the arid lifeless and empty baubles and trinkets strewn over the desert of our exhausted culture.

This is the great adventure that many began when they innocently and trustingly accepted long ago the Baltimore Catechism's simple definition of prayer: "Prayer is a lifting of the mind and heart to God." It is my hope and prayer that this brief offering may help many realize that our church, with its rituals, devotions, and practices, is a treasure trove of aids to an abiding awareness of the presence of God in our lives. Indeed, I hope to have shown that contemplative awareness of the sacred in which we are immersed is the normal fruit of our prayer life. The treasure is lying just beneath the rituals, images and formulas that we so easily take for granted as we go marching off in search of what we already possess in abundance. This brief introduction to contemplative prayer and living is offered in the hope that many will enter anew into that process and allow themselves to be taken along the journey to a loving union with the divine for which their heart is even now longing. The ongoing renewal of the church depends now on reclaiming our true contemplative and mystical heritage.

Recommended Reading

Contemplative Prayer and Mysticism

Maloney, George A., *The Mystery of Christ in You: The Mystical Vision of Saint Paul*. New York: Alba House, 1998.

Merton, Thomas, *Contemplative Prayer*. New York: Herder & Herder, 1969.

Sanford, John A., *Mystical Christianity: A Psychological Commentary on the Gospel of John*. New York: Crossroad, 1993.

Underhill, Evelyn, *Mysticism: A Study in the Nature and Development of Man's Spiritual Consiousness*. Oxford, England: Oneworld Publications Ltd., 1999.

Lectio Divina

Masini, Mario, *Lectio Divina: An Ancient Prayer That Is Ever New*. Edmurd C. Lane, translator. New York: Alba House, 1998.

Pennington, M. Basil, *Lectio Divina: Renewing the Ancient Practice of Praying the Scriptures.* New York: Crossroad, 1998.

Salvail, Ghislaine, *At the Crossroads of Scripture: An Introduction to Lectio Divina.* Paul Duggan, translator. Boston: Pauline Books and Media, 1996.

Centering Prayer

Keating, Thomas, *Contemplative Prayer: Traditional Christian Meditations for Opening to Divine Union*, Audio Cassette. Boulder, CO: Sounds True, 1995.

__________, *Intimacy With God.* New York: Crossroad, 1994.

__________, *Open Mind, Open Heart: The Contemplative Dimension of the Gospel.* Rockport, MA: Element, 1992.

Reininger, Gustave, ed., *Centering Prayer in Daily Life and Ministry.* New York: Continuum, 1998.

The Jesus Prayer

Ware, Kallistos, *The Power of the Name: The Jesus Prayer in Orthodox Spirituality*. Fairacres, Oxford: SLG Press, 1977.

Zaleski, Irma, *Living the Jesus Prayer*. New York: Continuum, 1998.

The Rosary

Vail, Anne and Caryll Houselander, *Joy of the Rosary: A Way Into Meditative Prayer*. Liguori, MO: Liguori Publications, 1998.

RAYMOND J. GUNZEL, SP, is a member of the Servants of Paraclete. Ordained in 1969, he has spent his priestly ministry in therapeutic treatment centers as spiritual director, instructor, and administrator. He has given retreats and workshops on contemplative prayer. Father Gunzel is presently on staff at the Father Fitzgerald Center for Retreats and Conferences in Jamez Springs, New Mexico.